ASHINGTON AFC IN THE FOOTBALL LEAGUE

A Complete Record 1921-29

Garth Dykes

A *SoccerData* Publication

Published in Great Britain by Tony Brown,
4 Adrian Close, Beeston, Nottingham NG9 6FL.
Telephone 0115 973 6086. E-mail soccer@innotts.co.uk
First published 2011

Cover design by Bob Budd.

Archive photographs © Colorsport and others from the collections of Bryan Milne and the author.

DEDICATION

To Clara with love

Printed and bound by 4edge Limited, Hockley, Essex
www.4edge.co.uk

ISBN: 978-1-905891-48-1

AUTHOR'S PREFACE

As one whose football education began on the terraces of Oldham Athletic in the immediate post-war years, I have retained a lifelong interest in the game with particularly fond memories of the many Third Division North matches that I attended at Boundary Park. It is, therefore, my pleasure and privilege to document the League history of Ashington AFC, former members of the Northern Section. In tracing the history and players of the Colliers during their relatively short lived spell as a Football League club one has come to appreciate that finances, or lack of same, has been an ever-present concern, both then and now, for clubs in the lower reaches of the Football League. The custodians of the Ashington club from 1921 to 1929 were certainly swimming against the tide. At the advent of each season, preparations were hampered by lack of cash resources and mounting debts. The majority of players were by necessity recruited from local non-League clubs, and many played as amateurs. It was of great credit to the Directorate that the club managed to remain competitive throughout their Football League years, and the history of those times, and the details of the players who wore the Colliers' colours during their eight years in the Northern Section of the League are recorded in these pages. Researches into our national game are ongoing, and amplification of information on any of the players who have qualified for inclusion into this book will be warmly welcomed. I can be contacted via the publisher.

Garth Dykes
Leicester,
April 2011

ACKNOWLEDGEMENTS

My thanks, as ever, go to Jim Creasy and Mike Davage for their considerable help during the twelve months that I have spent on this project. I am also most grateful for the assistance of Bryan Milne, who has been most generous with his time and encyclopaedic knowledge of all matters relating to football in the North East. I am indebted to several others for their willing help throughout this project; an especial thank you to Peter Holme, Research Officer of the Football Museum at Preston, for access to their records, and to Robin Peake, a MRes student at the University of Ulster, whose outstandingly thorough research and documentation of the life and career of Patrick O'Connell (Ashington AFC 1920-22) cannot be over praised. I am also grateful to Michael Braham, Stephen Byrne, Mike Jackman, Paul Joannou, Sue O'Connell, Paul Plowman, Gordon Small, and my dear sister Hilary for her unfailing help. Paul Ternant of the Woodhorn Museum and Archive at Ashington, and Richard Hodges of the Heritage Team at Newcastle City Library are thanked for their assistance in tracing match reports. Last, but by no means least, my thanks as ever to my dear partner Ann for her unfailing help and encouragement.

The 1926-27 team at Walsall, 6th September 1926. Back: Chester, Ferguson, J Dalkin, Elliott, Hamilton, Warrell (trainer), Chipperfield. Front: Malloy, Robinson, Johnson, Randall, Laverick, Price

A SHORT HISTORY OF ASHINGTON A.F.C.

PRE-LEAGUE

The growth of football in the Ashington area is closely linked to the prosperity of the Northumberland coalfield in the latter part of the 19th century. The club is thought to have followed on from Ashington Rising Star, formed in 1883, and who played in the Northumberland Challenge Cup from 1885. Joannou and Candlish, in *Pioneers of the North* point out that the interest in the activities of more senior clubs at Shankhouse and Morpeth undoubtedly led to clubs being formed in other local towns. Ashington first entered the FA Cup in 1888, losing to Elswick Rangers – indeed, they had a long wait until their first win in the competition, which came in 1906-07.

The Football League was formed in 1888. Its commercial success led to a proliferation of junior leagues, one of which was the Northern Alliance, formed in 1890. The club had one season in the Alliance, in 1892-93. Financial difficulties seemed to have forced them back to a non-league status, though played Kendal and Willington Athletic in the FA Amateur Cup of 1893-94. After this loss of interest, a fresh start was discussed in May 1895 and the club joined the East Northumberland League for 1895-96. They were back in the Alliance for 1902-03 to 1913-14, finishing as runners-up in 1905-06, 1910-11 and 1911-12. The club's first honour was the Northumberland Challenge Bowl in 1912-13, followed by the Alliance league title in 1913-14. They then joined the North Eastern League for 1914-15. The difficulties encountered by the outbreak of the First World War brought an end to most football in the North East, until the North Eastern League resumed in 1919.

There had been considerable discussion since before the War about the Football League forming a third division by adding the Southern League clubs. When this finally happened in 1920, immediate discussions took place over the possibility of a northern division. With no comparable "Northern League" it was left for individual clubs to apply for membership of the new League. Ashington, along with fellow North Eastern League clubs Darlington, Durham City and Hartlepools United decided to make the step up. They would have been buoyed by their first Northumberland Senior Cup win in 1920-21.

THE FOOTBALL LEAGUE

At the close of the 1920-21 season, Ashington A.F.C. purchased the freehold of their ground from the Duke of Portland, and £6,000 was spent in remodelling the enclosure, the holding capacity being increased to approximately 25,000 spectators. Alterations included the front row for the spectators being sunk by some three feet below the playing surface, which was levelled and re-laid. The covered stand was reconstructed and erected on a brick foundation. It featured fine dressing rooms for the teams and offices for the management. A year earlier, the ground had been terraced on three sides, and as the club embarked on its great adventure as members of the Football League, the club boasted some of the best facilities in the Northern Section of Division Three. Always a strong team in the North Eastern League, Ashington were expected to make a name for themselves in Division Three. The club had very attractive opposition for their opening fixture, Grimsby Town were one of the original members of the League when the Second Division was formed in 1892-93, and had spent two years in the First Division between 1901-03. An attendance of around 8,000 spectators attended the opening match, and prior to the kick-off, a brief opening ceremony was conducted by Mr Ridley Warham, managing director of the Ashington Coal Company. A new flag was unfurled, embodying the colours of the club, and this was presented by Mrs E. Main, wife of one of the club's directors. A vote of thanks was then moved by local Labour leader Mr J.M. Gillians.

The Ashington team for their debut in the Football League lined up as follows:
Davidson; Bradford, Buxton; Featherstone, O'Connell (Captain), Barber; Foster, Dickinson, Thompson, McGill, Brayson.

It was unfortunate that Tom Robertson, the leading scorer of the previous season was unavailable due to injury, but the team managed without him, a single goal by Dickinson was enough to secure maximum points although the unfortunate goal scorer was later carried from the field after being knocked out. Throughout the whole of their first season the Colliers lacked consistency but they finished in tenth place and enjoyed a run in the FA Cup that came to a halt at Millwall, a game that was witnessed by 20,000 spectators.

Sadly, the advent of their second season was anticipated with anxiety, a four-figure loss on the previous season brought about a re-organisation of finances.

A postcard from the Ashington secretary to the Football League, January 1923

Wary of a heavy bill for wages, a number of experienced players were transferred in the close season, with most of the new men coming from the local leagues. The season opened with a 6-1 defeat at Wigan Borough but after seven matches the side were fifth in the table. A slump of epic proportions then saw the side win just once in a run of sixteen matches from early November to mid February. A late rally gave some hope of avoiding a re-election application, but other results on the final day left them in the bottom two. The fact that the Northern section was extended by a further two clubs (Doncaster Rovers and New Brighton) probably did no harm to both re-applicants, both Ashington and Durham City receiving maximum votes.

A further drop in average home attendances had resulted in a loss of £400 on the season's workings. There were, however, signs of improvement in the colliery areas and the 1923-24 season saw an almost complete change in the playing personnel of the team. Much of the lack of success in the previous season was addressed by the signing of players with a more robust physique. The lightly-built team of the previous campaign had performed well in the early months, but the advent of heavier pitches had exposed shortcomings in the squad. With no fewer than nine new players in the side for the season's opener at Wrexham, an unsurprising lack of cohesion led to a heavy 4-0 defeat at the Racecourse. Two days later, however, League newcomers Doncaster Rovers were beaten 3-1 at Portland Park and by November 3rd, with an excellent eight-match unbeaten run safely negotiated, the side stood fifth in the table. Some progress in the FA Cup competition was achieved with wins against non-League opponents Bishop Auckland and Carlisle United, followed by the sixth qualifying round victory against Hartlepools United. This set up the plum tie against Aston Villa at Portland Park. A 7-1 home defeat by Wolverhampton Wanderers on the previous Saturday could have done little for the team's morale or confidence and Villa, the eventually finalists, (who lost 2-0 against Newcastle United at Wembley) had few problems in overcoming the Colliers 5-1 before a record crowd of 11,837. League form dipped in late season but despite recording only two wins in the final nine matches an eighth place finish was achieved; a placing that would not be bettered under Football League auspices. A profit of £297 was recorded, a result largely due to the increased success in the FA Cup, and the formation of a Supporter's Club, comprised of both sexes, that proved to be a great help to the management.

Many changes were again evident in the playing ranks for season 1924-25. Notable among the departures were Hoffman to Darlington, Page to Lincoln City, Pigg to Queens Park Rangers and Relph to Brentford. The most notable signing was Ferguson, a full-back, whom the club had transferred to Chelsea four years earlier. There were four new players on view in the season's opener, a 2-1 win against Chesterfield at Portland Park, this was followed by a 2-0 win against Doncaster Rovers and a goal-less draw at Durham City. Sadly, the bright start was not maintained. The side lost four consecutive matches in the month of October, and they were without a League win in November. Hopes of some progress in the FA Cup competition were dashed when the Colliers were disqualified for fielding an ineligible player, John Anderson, in the replayed tie against Hartlepools United on November 19th. Following a 7-1 thrashing at Bradford Park Avenue on December 17th the team rallied, remaining unbeaten in their next seven matches. They remained in the top half of the table until a late season slump in April saw them finish in tenth position, thanks to two victories in the last three matches of the season. The Reserve side took the season's honours, winning the championship of the Northern Alliance with a record number of goals scored.

The principal departures in the 1925 close season were Ritchie and Tubb, both of whom migrated to Barrow. New signings included Elliott, Scotswood's goalkeeper, who had previous League experience with Preston North End. Three new forwards, Randall and Dalkin (ex Bedlington United) and Turnbull (Newport County) were all expected to develop. The trio did not disappoint in a season when the side were off to an excellent start, a six-match unbeaten run including a 5-1 victory against Nelson at Portland Park, Randall scoring a hat trick on his debut. The side maintained the club in the top half of the League throughout much of the season, although the campaign ended in disappointment. A victory at Chesterfield on the season's final day could have taken the Colliers to the dizzy heights of fifth, but the heaviest defeat of the season ensued, the 6-1 thrashing leaving the team in ninth place.

At the outset of season 1926-27, the *Athletic News* noted that the whole of the Colliers players were Northumberland born, apart from James Price, captain of the side in the past two seasons, and new signing Henry Marsh from Usworth Colliery. The season commenced with a 4-0 defeat at New Brighton, but two draws and a win by 4-1 at Wigan Borough lifted hopes. In the next seven League matches, however, the side gathered only three points and shipped an alarming total of 24 goals. The FA Cup brought some relief, however, victories of 2-1 were achieved against Stockton and Nelson, earning the side a home tie against Second Division Nottingham Forest. At this point of the season Ashington had not been beaten at home, and a crowd of 9,242 saw Ferguson win the toss and kick off against the wind. Rain was falling heavily and the surface of the playing area was very slippery. The Colliers forced three corner kicks in quick succession but Forest settled and the Colliers were indebted to goalkeeper Ridley who saved smartly from Burton and Stocks. An injury to Ted Ferguson after about 25 minutes play left him a limping passenger on the wing, and within minutes Forest scored the first of two goals that took them through to Round Four. The Colliers' season literally fell apart following this defeat, no fewer than 13 consecutive League matches failing to realise a victory. Home attendances by this point had slumped to less than 2,000 spectators, but the advent of centre-forward Ball, a late season signing from Seghill Colliery Welfare, steered the side away from the re-election zone. His return of 10 goals in 12 matches being a major factor in the team's final placing of sixteenth.

The depression in the northern coalfields continued to have a big effect on the finances of the club and despite an income of £1,000 in transfer fees received, a loss on the year's working amounted to £225. The inability of the club to pay summer wages left the playing ranks far from complete with the new 1927-28 season a matter of two weeks away. Not surprisingly, the side conceded 25 goals in six matches in September, and it was not until the fifteenth match of the season that the side took maximum points in a 3-0 win against Tranmere Rovers at Portland Park. Bottom of the League and out of the FA Cup by the end of November, things took a much needed upturn when Nelson were beaten 5-1 at Seedhill on December 3rd – the team's first victory on the road – and this was followed by a 1-0 home win against Barrow and a 1-1 draw at Rotherham United. Results in the second half of the season showed some improvement, thanks largely to the increased firepower of the attack. Johnson, Ball and Watson were all prominent, and although Sam Ball had the misfortune to fracture his leg at Durham City on April 18th, two draws and a 6-0 win against Rotherham United ensured survival for another season. With no income from the transfer of players and the ever decreasing attendances, the Colliers experienced their worst ever loss of the season's working - £1,541 14s 4d. With total debts amounting to £3,750 hanging over their heads, the Directorate were again obliged to tread cautiously when recruiting for the new season. For the most part, the new players engaged were locals, but a new departure was the signing of the former Burnley centre-half and ex-Collier George Thompson as trainer-coach.

The 1928-29 season opened with a 2-1 defeat at Southport, but home wins against Darlington (4-2) and Rochdale (2-1) followed. Sadly, the improvement did not last, five matches without a victory immediately followed. A crushing 8-2 home defeat against Bradford City was immediately followed by the Yorkshire club's signing of the Colliers' outside-left James Randall. The transfer fee was £400, with provision for a further £100 if Bradford City won promotion, which they did. The Colliers meanwhile were going in the opposite direction, marooned at the foot of the table throughout much of the season. They were literally "hit for six" in February 1929 when Doncaster Rovers won a high scoring encounter at Portland Park. The home side scored four goals for only the second time during the season, but the Rovers scored seven, star centre-forward Tom Keetley netting a double hat-trick. The lowest crowd of the season at that point numbered just 729 spectators. Despite the last three League matches all being played at home, the team managed to win only once in their final eight matches and finished at the bottom of the League. With an average attendance of less than 2,000 for the season their re-election application was made more in hope than expectation. In early June 1929 the axe fell, the Colliers received only 14 votes and were replaced by York City. Fellow applicants Hartlepools United were comfortably re-elected with 33 votes.

AFTER THE FOOTBALL LEAGUE

The obvious place for the club was a return to the North Eastern League. Most players on the books in 1928-29 were released and the club had to look for new players. The reserve team had been relegated to Division Two of the North Eastern League at the end of 1928-29, and the club found itself 'starting again' in this division. They were back in the top flight for 1930-31.

There were Northumberland Senior Cup wins in 1932-33 and 1938-39 before the next World War again brought the formal competitions to an end, though various war-time competitions were played throughout the 1939-1945 period. In the immediate post-war years, Ashington remained in the North Eastern League, with a best-place third finish in 1955-56 and 1957-58.

From 1958 to 1970, Ashington's fortunes in football mirrored the search for a stable league platform for clubs in the north-east. The North Eastern League had been formed largely for the reserve teams of Football League clubs, so when these teams left in 1958 to form the North Regional League the North Eastern League was forced to close down. Ashington and other clubs found themselves in the Midland League, which had also lost clubs to the North Regional League. As might be expected, the travel costs made this alliance uneconomic and the northern clubs formed the Northern Counties League in 1960. Ashington had two seasons in this league but then joined the re-formed North Eastern League; this only lasted for two seasons and 1964-65 found the club in the Wearside League. After one season it was off to the North Regional League for three seasons.

1968 saw the foundation of the Northern Premier League, an attempt to gather together the best clubs in the north of England. Founder members came from the Cheshire, Lancashire Combination, Midland, North Regional and West Midlands (Regional) leagues, with invitations offered to those clubs with the best records in the previous three seasons. Ashington were one of three clubs selected from the North Regional League, along with Gateshead and South Shields. The bottom three clubs had to retire from the League at the end of the first season, Ashington being one of them after finishing 18th out of 20. So 1969-70 found them back in the Northern Alliance, a league they had last graced in 1913-14 (although the reserves spent most of the post-war years in this league).

Meanwhile, sailing serenely on in large untroubled waters was the Northern League. This league started alongside the North Eastern League in 1889. Although down to 6 clubs at one stage, the league hosted clubs such as Middlesbrough, Darlington and Sheffield United, who all went on to long Football League careers. In the 1920s and 1930s, clubs such as Crook Town and Bishop Auckland won its championship. By the 1970s, Blyth Spartans and Spennymoor United had come to the fore. Ashington's first season in the Northern League was 1970-71, and here they remain. The League split into two divisions in 1982, with Ashington subsequently spending two spells in the lower division.

The club moved to a new ground at Woodhorn Lane in the summer of 2008. Portland Park was used throughout their time in the Football League. It opened in 1909 and was named after the Duke of Portland, who owned the land. After League football had ended a dog track was added to the stadium, which was later also used for speedway. A 1940s postcard (below) shows the dog track, with the original grandstand visible on the right. The highest attendance came in 1950, when 13,199 packed in to see the cup-tie with Rochdale. The early club had played at the Recreation Ground, close to the colliery, and played one season 1908-09 in Station Road on a field rented from the Co-op.

The town and the football club are rightly proud of the many local men who have had success in the game, notably the Charlton brothers (Bobby and Jack), Jimmy Adamson (Footballer of the Year in 1962) and Jackie Milburn. Since many of these men fall outside our scope of *Ashington AFC in the Football League* we are happy to direct you to the "history" section of the club's excellent web site at www.ashingtonafc.com.

An early group from 1898-99, players unknown

1914, players unknown

1922-23. Back: Tubb, Featherstone, Davidson, Hamilton, Hetherington (trainer), Burton. Front: Soulsby, Hunter, T Robertson, Foster, Price.

1925-26. Back: Randall, G Thompson, Collings (treasurer), Ferguson, Elliott, Hamilton, Chipperfield, Gregory (secretary), Hetherington (trainer). Front: Turnbull, Ward, Johnson, Carlton, Watson, Price.

1928-29. Back: Price, Wilson, G Robson, Latimer, Thompson, Chipperfield, Stephenson. Front: Alexander, Harris, Johnson, Carlton, G Richardson.

THE FOOTBALL LEAGUE PLAYERS OF ASHINGTON A.F.C. 1921-29

NOTES ON THE TEXT

For each player I have attempted to provide the following information: full names, recognised playing position, height and weight, date and place of birth, and date and place of death. It should be mentioned here that the dates of birth and death of some players have been culled from registers that only record such events in three-month periods. Hence the use (for instance) of 'January quarter 1923', which denotes a span of January/ February/March of that year. Also included are each player's Ashington debut, full career and biographical details, and a breakdown of appearances made and goals scored. Every player who appeared in a Football League match or an FA Cup-tie has been included.

ABBREVIATIONS

These have been kept to a minimum and are those in general use in works of this type:

App/s	Appearance/s
cs	close season
gl/s	Goal/s
q.v. (quod vide)	denoting a cross reference
FA	The Football Association
FL	The Football League
WW1	The First World War (1914-18)
WW2	The Second World War (1939–45)

ALEXANDER, John William

Outside-right   5' 10"   12st 0lbs
Born: Percy Main, 22 August 1899
Died: Bury, January quarter 1976
Career: Percy Main Amateurs. Preston Colliery. ASHINGTON amateur July 1922. Hull City amateur June, professional July 1926. ASHINGTON July 1928. Workington July 1929. Bury November 1929, fee £250. Workington August 1930. Throckley Welfare September 1934. Wills Sports (Mitcham) later in September 1934.
Debut v Chesterfield (h) 30.8.24, won 2-1
A former miner and elder brother of Stanley Alexander who assisted five different League clubs in the inter war period, scoring 78 goals in 278 matches. John's career was modest by comparison, as he made no senior appearances beyond those in Ashington's colours. Considered one of the fastest wingmen of his time, he was odds-on favourite to win the famous Powderhill Sprint at Edinburgh on New Year's Day 1927, but finished disappointingly in third place. He first assisted the Colliers, as an amateur, in seven matches in season 1924-25, returning as a professional in 1928-29 to appear in 29 League matches and one FA Cup-tie. His solitary goal opened the scoring in a 3-2 victory against Tranmere Rovers on 13th April 1929 in what proved to be Ashington's final win in the Football League. They finished at the foot of the Northern Section table with 23 points from 42 matches and were not re-elected
Appearances: FL: 36 apps 1 gl FAC: 1 app 0 gls Total: 37 apps 1 gl

ANDERSON, John

Outside-right
Born: Hedleyhope, near Crook, December 1900
Career: Crook Town. Workington August 1922. Shildon (trial) September 1922. West Stanley. ASHINGTON amateur cs 1924, registered for FL matches 21st November 1924, registration cancelled February 1925. West Stanley.
Debut v Hartlepools United, FAC 4Q Replay (h) 19.11.24, won 2-0
Anderson's debut for Ashington led to their disqualification from the FA Cup. An injury

early in the game saw the former West Stanley wingman miss the remainder of the first half, his absence upsetting the combination of the forwards. His return, later in the second half, saw a marked improvement, two goals from Gardner securing victory for the home side. The Colliers were drawn to entertain Bishop Auckland in the fifth qualifying round on November 29th, but it was subsequently revealed that Anderson had played two days prior to being registered, and was therefore an ineligible player, leading to Ashington's disqualification. Four days later, Anderson's second and final appearance was a league match against the same opponents, and in a disappointing display by the home side, Hartlepools were fully deserving of their 3-0 victory.

Appearances: FL: 1 app 0 gls FAC: 1 app 0 gls
Total: 2 apps 0 gls

ARCHER, George Thompson

Centre or Right-half   5' 10"   12st 2lbs
Born: Corbridge, near Hexham, 19 August 1899
Died: Morpeth, April 1993

Career: Hexham Town. ASHINGTON June 1922; re-signed September 1924 and retained for season 1925-26.
Debut v Wigan Borough (h) 2.9.22, won 2-1
A reserve centre or wing half-back of sturdy build, Archer's best run in the first team was five consecutive matches in September 1922 when the team won three, lost one and one match was drawn. Thereafter his first team opportunities were infrequent, although it has to be said that the persistent team changes made throughout the season brought no success. A winning combination proved elusive, the side finishing next-to-bottom of the table, and were faced with a re-election application. Archer was re-signed in September 1924 and retained for the following season when he made a final League appearance in the 1-1 draw with Southport at Portland Park on September 26th, 1925.

Appearances: FL: 12 apps 0 gls Total: 12 apps 0 gls

BAILEY, Herbert Albert

Left-back   5' 10"   11st 10lbs
Born: Amble, Northumberland, 7 November 1894
Died: Durham North, January quarter 1955
Career: Amble. ASHINGTON May 1922.
Debut v Barrow (h) 23.12.22, lost 2-6
Reserve team full-back Herbert Bailey had a tough baptism in League football. One of seven team changes for the visit of Barrow, he was directly opposed to Cyril Matthews, widely recognised as one of the best wingmen operating in the Northern Section. At the outset, a missed kick by the former Amble defender let in a Barrow forward who fortunately spurned his opportunity by shooting wide. The reprieve did not last long, however, despite a rearrangement that took Featherstone to his usual position of left-back with Bailey being moved up into the middle line. The final outcome, a 6-2 defeat, was not the worst home defeat suffered by the Colliers. Wolverhampton Wanderers won 7-1 at Portland Park in January 1924, while other heavy defeats at home came against Bradford City, 8-2 in October 1928 and 7-4 against Doncaster Rovers in February 1929.

Appearances: FL: 2 apps 0 gls Total: 2 apps 0 gls

BAINBRIDGE, John Taylor

Outside-right
Born: North Shields, 17 August 1900
Died: Gateshead, 20 December 1945
Career: ASHINGTON amateur August 1922, registered for FL matches December 1922. Gateshead Town August 1923. Birtley August 1924.
Debut v Bradford Park Avenue (a) 21.4.23, lost 0-3
A late replacement for James Soulsby on the Colliers right-wing, John Bainbridge was promoted from the "A" Team to make his debut in the return fixture at Bradford Park Avenue. It proved a tough baptism against a team who mounted a serious challenge for promotion from the Northern Section at the first attempt, following successive relegations. The Park Avenue side nearly succeeded, finishing second to Nelson, when only one team was promoted from the Division. By contrast, and despite a late rally when the team took eight points from their final six matches, Ashington finished 19th in the table and, along with Durham City, were obliged to seek re-election.
Appearances: FL: 1 app 0 gls Total: 1 app 0 gls

BALL, Samuel

Centre-forward/Inside-right
5' 9"   11st 3lbs
Born: Newsham, Northumberland, 21 August 1907
Died: Carlisle, April 1984
Career: Seghill Colliery Welfare. Blyth Spartans. New Delaval Villa. West Stanley August 1925. Chelsea (trial) November 1925. West Stanley July 1926. Seghill Colliery Welfare January 1927. ASHINGTON March 1927, and re-signed January 1929. New Deleval Villa September 1929. Blyth Spartans January 1932.
Debut v Accrington Stanley (a) 19.3.27, lost 0-3
Introduced from non-League football as a replacement for leading scorer Bill Harris who, earlier in the same month, had left to join Huddersfield Town. Ball was quickly into his stride, scoring ten goals in his first twelve appearances. His total included "doubles" in victories against Barrow, Crewe

Alexandra and Southport, results that lifted the Colliers from the lower reaches of the table to the relative comfort of sixteenth place. Retained for the following season, Ball began by scoring four goals in a pre-season practice match, but after scoring seven goals in fourteen matches he lost his place at centre-forward to George Johnson and requested a transfer, which was granted on 16th January 1928. On the same date, however, he was reintroduced at inside-right and, two weeks later, Ball and Johnson both scored hat-tricks in a 6-3 win against Wigan Borough. The pair had worked well in tandem, but Ball was not retained, having had the misfortune to break his leg at Durham City on 18th April. Although re-signed when recovered from his injury in January 1929, on this occasion he was unable to lift the side, his five appearances yielding only one point and an adverse goal difference of one scored, seventeen conceded.
Appearances: FL: 44 apps 23 gls FAC: 2 apps 2 gls Total: 46 apps 25 gls

BARBER, John Foster

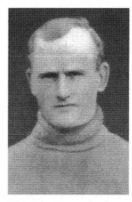

Left-half
5' 8½"   11st 7lbs
Born: Felling, Gateshead, 5 September 1893
Died: Felling, Gateshead, October quarter 1969
Career: Washington United 1912. Seaton Delaval 1913. Burnley August 1914.
Wartime guest player with Lancaster United (Barrow & District League) 1916-17.
ASHINGTON during season 1919-20.
Workington June 1922.
Debut v Grimsby Town (h) 27.8.21, won 1-0
Whilst a Seaton Delaval player, John Barber represented the Northern Alliance team against the champions (Ashington) at Portland Park in 1914. The League X1 won by three clear goals, Barber scoring a hat-trick. Burnley officials who were present at the match were successful in obtaining his

signature. He captained Burnley's Central League side during the war and also made guest appearances with Lancaster United, for whom he scored 29 goals in season 1916-17. During Ashington's North Eastern League days he was selected to represent the League against Middlesbrough Reserves. During his stay with the Colliers he occupied every outfield position, but his best performances were made in the middle line. Equally effective in defence and attack, he was said to be "Always in the thick of it, and always as cool at the end of the game as at the commencement."
Appearances: FL: 23 apps 3 gls Total: 23 apps 3 gls

BEILBY, Norman William

Right-half
Born: Hartlepool, 21 September 1900
Died: Gateshead, 25 September 1988
Career: Wood Skinner's. ASHINGTON November 1921. Low Fell August 1922. The Wednesday May 1923. Wardley Colliery September 1926. Ravenswood Welfare October 1926. Newcastle Blue Star September 1930.
Debut v Halifax Town (h) 4.2.22, won 3-1
In his two appearances as deputy for John Barber, Norman Beilby stepped up from reserve team football and proved a useful auxiliary, but was not considered ready for an extended run in the side, despite a policy bordering on "all change" in the middle line. No fewer than seven different players being fielded at right-half during the season. A second opportunity in League football came with his move from Low Fell to The Wednesday in May 1923, but he failed to reach senior level at Hillsborough.
Appearances: FL: 2 apps 0 gls Total: 2 apps 0 gls

BEST, Edward

Left-back   5' 9"   12st 0lbs
Born: West Mickley, 27 September 1899
Died: North Central, July quarter 1975
Career: Mickley. ASHINGTON July 1926. Mickley February 1930. Chopwell Institute August 1930. Mickley (trial) August 1932.
Debut v Lincoln City (h) 10.9.27, lost 4-5
After a full season spent at reserve level, Best emerged from the shadow of the former England Schools International left-back George Hamilton to make his league debut in early season 1927-28. He was one of four changes made for the visit of Lincoln City, but the problems in defence continued, in the first seven matches of the season the side leaked 28 goals, and despite some improvement, the season's total of goals against stood at 103, with only four "clean sheets" maintained throughout. Best nevertheless retained the left-back position for a lengthy run of consecutive appearances, finally ending with the 3-1 home defeat by Southport on Christmas Eve 1927. Best's brother, Jerry, was Coventry City's goalkeeper for six seasons after the Great War, appearing in 236 League and Cup matches.
Appearances: FL: 17 apps 0 gls FAC: 2 apps 0 gls Total: 19 apps 0 gls

BRADFORD, Alexander

Right-back   5' 8½"   10st 9lbs
Born: Broomhill, July quarter 1892
Died: Broomhill, April quarter 1963
Career: Broomhill FC. East Chevington. Sunderland. ASHINGTON signed before FL entry and re-registered for FL matches July 1921. Amble October 1927. East Chevington Black Watch. North Broomhill Welfare January 1930. Eshott FC circa 1930. Hauxley United (Northern Junior Cup finalists).
Debut v Grimsby Town (h) 27.8.21, won 1-0
After appearing regularly at right-back throughout the Colliers' first season in the Football League, Alex Bradford lost his first team place following a heavy 6-1 defeat at Wigan Borough on the opening day of the following season. A full-back pairing of Mahon and Featherstone was introduced for the return fixture which resulted in a 2-1 victory for the Colliers and the pair remained undisturbed for much of the rest of the campaign. Alex Bradford's single goal was the result of a successful conversion of a penalty kick, and it earned his team the points in a 1-0 win against Darlington at Portland Park in April 1922.
Appearances: FL: 38 apps 1 gl FAC: 3 apps 0 gls Total: 41 apps 1 gl

BRADLEY, William

Goalkeeper
6' 0"   11st 5lbs
Born: Wardley, Gateshead, 1 March 1893
Career: Dunston Wednesday. Fatfield Albion. Jarrow Caledonians October 1911. Portsmouth March 1912, fee £100.
Jarrow August 1913. Newcastle United April 1914, fee £300. Wartime guest player with Scotswood December 1915. ASHINGTON September 1927. North Shields February 1930, subsequently a director of the club from March 1933.
Debut v Lincoln City (h) 10.9.27, lost 4-5
Bill Bradley joined Portsmouth in time to assist them to promotion from the Second Division of the Southern League in season 1911-12, when they finished runners-up to Merthyr Town on goal average. His transfer to Newcastle United initially cast him in a reserve role, with the durable Scottish International Jimmy Lawrence firmly established in goal. It was not until after the Great War – during which he served in the Tank Corps – that the tall and slim goalkeeper made his first senior appearance in a 1-0 home win against Preston North End on November 1st, 1919 and he eventually totalled 133 League and 10 FA Cup appearances for the Magpies. In season 1923-24 he was replaced in mid term by veteran goalkeeper Sandy Mutch and was very fortunate to appear in his place in the FA Cup Final against Aston Villa when Mutch suffered a severe knee injury in the week prior to the Wembley final. A daring and often brilliant goalkeeper, his talents were utilised to the full behind a leaky Ashington defence that had conceded sixteen goals in four matches prior to his arrival. Outside of the game, Bradley ran a hen ranch and later was a newsagent in North Shields.
Appearances: FL: 36 apps 0 gls FAC: 1 app 0 gls Total: 37 apps 0 gls
Honours: Newcastle United, FA Cup winners 1924

BRANNAN, Frank

Right-half   5' 10½" 11st 8lbs
Born: Walker, Newcastle-on-Tyne
Career: Chester-le-Street. Shildon July 1924. ASHINGTON August 1925. Walker Celtic September 1926. Spen Black & White August 1927.
Debut v Accrington Stanley (a) 31.10.25, lost 1-2

Recruiting by the Colliers during the first week of August 1925 included the re-signing of their regular backs, Ted Ferguson and George Hamilton. They also secured the centre-half of Shildon, Frank Brannan, who was said to have made over fifty appearances for the Durham North-East Club in the previous season. Prior to that, he had played regularly with Chester-le-Street in the same competition. With James Price so firmly established as first team pivot, Brannan spent his season in the reserves, aside from four consecutive outings at right-half, spanning October and November 1925. No fewer than eight different players were tried on the right flank of the middle line during the season. Ironically, it was not until centre-forward George Johnson was switched into the position that results improved, his constructive work and prompting a key element in the team's elevation to ninth place in the final table.
Appearances: FL: 4 apps 0 gls Total: 4 apps 0 gls

BRAYSON, Joseph Hayes

Outside-left   5' 9"   11st 0lbs
Born: Denton Burn, Newcastle-on-Tyne, 12 December 1901
Died: Denton Burn, Newcastle-on-Tyne, 13 May 1970
Career: Newburn. Wallsend. South Shields December 1919. Newburn June 1920. ASHINGTON May 1921. Scotswood June 1922. Hull City April 1926. Annfield Plain July 1928. West Stanley August 1930.
Debut v Grimsby Town (h) 27.8.21, won 1-0
The Colliers fielded an entirely new forward line for their debut in the Football League, the chief goal scorer of the previous season, Tom Robertson, being unavailable due to injury. Brayson was guilty of wasting a glorious chance in the first half when he shot just wide of the upright from close range. Although he had a hand in the deciding goal netted by Joe Dickinson, he spent the remainder of the season in reserve, apart from a late season appearance at Chesterfield as deputy for Tom McCloud. The Colliers won 1-0 at Saltergate and were indebted to goalkeeper Shepherd whose heroics included the saving of a penalty in the first half of the match.
Appearances: FL: 2 apps 0 gls Total: 2 apps 0 gls

BURTON, Ridley

Half-back   5' 9"   12st 2lbs
Born: Chopington, Northumberland, 21 December 1893
Died: Seaton Sluice, Northumberland, 28 October 1974
Career: Gateshead Rodsley. Seaton Delaval. Middlesbrough (trial). Windy Nook. Newcastle City February 1914. Close Works (Gateshead). Grimsby Town July 1919. West Stanley July 1920. Birmingham (trial). ASHINGTON July 1921. Chester-le-Street July 1924. Preston Colliery August 1925. Subsequently played in the USA.

Debut v Wigan Borough (a) 26.8.22, lost 1-6
Once described as "A second Charlie Roberts" when displaying his talents in Tyneside junior football. This was high praise indeed for a junior, as Roberts was an England International and considered one of the best pivots in the history of the game. In due course, Burton followed Robert's path when he joined Grimsby Town. While both players spent about a season with the Mariners, Roberts left to join Manchester United, subsequently winning two League championships and the FA Cup, Ridley Burton, however, departed Blundell Park to spend a season of Northern Section football with Ashington, having failed to fulfil his undoubted early potential.
Appearances: FL: 29 apps 1 gl FAC: 1 app 0 gls Total: 30 apps 1 gl

BUXTON, Stephen

Left-back
5' 6"   11st 8lbs
Born: South Bank, 3 February 1888
Died: South Bank, 21 April 1953
Career: South Bank. Brentford August 1908. Oldham Athletic August 1911, fee £425. Darlington May 1913. Wartime guest player with Oldham Athletic, Chesterfield Municipal and Blyth Spartans. ASHINGTON July 1920. Workington 1922. South Bank Gasworks amateur May 1924. South Bank Committee member June 1935. Debut v Grimsby Town
(h) 27.8.21, won 1 – 0
A regular with Brentford, where he missed only three matches in as many seasons, Steve Buxton cost First Division Oldham Athletic a considerable fee in August 1911. Although small for a defender he received fulsome praise from the *Athletic News* correspondent, following the match between Oldham Athletic and Manchester City, shortly after his arrival at Boundary Park in

October 1911. "I greatly admired the play of Buxton. For a man of his inches he is a truly remarkable player, speedy, a clever and judicious tackler, a fine kick with either foot, and, above all, scrupulously fair." Sadly, his immense promise was cruelly cut short by a serious knee injury after just four matches in season 1912-13. His progress was further disrupted by the outbreak of World War One, during which he served in the Royal Army Medical Corps. Arriving at Ashington prior to Football League entry, he was selected to represent the North Eastern League versus the Central League in January 1921. Reported to be "A tower of strength" at left back in the early months of the Colliers first season of League football, he was unfortunately sidelined by injury for some weeks but recovered to end the season with a run of twelve consecutive appearances. Earlier in his career, Buxton won representative honours, playing for London against Birmingham, and he was also selected as reserve for the Southern League representative X1. Outside of the game, he was a Middlesbrough master builder.
Appearances: FL: 24 apps 0 gls Total: 24 apps 0 gls

CARLTON, John

Inside-forward/Wing-half
5' 7"   10st 6lbs
Born: Ashington, 29 January 1902
Died: Ashington, April quarter 1983
Career: Pegswood. ASHINGTON trial August 1925, amateur 12 November 1925, professional 26 November 1925. Frickley Colliery June 1929. ASHINGTON August 1931. Bedlington United January 1934.
Debut v Bradford Park Avenue (a) 14.11.25, lost 0-1
A lengthy association with the Colliers commenced with trials in August 1925, followed by a professional contract after a brief, two-week spell on amateur forms. Able to occupy either berth at inside-forward or wing-half, and with a capacity for hard work, he played fairly regularly in the first team in all seasons apart from 1926-27. Ironically, his best season proved to be Ashington's last as a

Football League club. In 27 League outings, Carlton scored eight goals. Typical of the season, however, was his scoring of a hat-trick against Doncaster Rovers in late February 1929, when the Colliers lost 4-7 before a 'gate' of just 729 spectators at Portland Park.
Appearances: FL: 67 apps 11 gls FAC: 2 apps 0 gls Total: 69 apps 11 gls

CHARLTON, Thomas

Left-half   5' 11"   12st 5lbs
Born: West Sleekburn, January quarter 1907
Career: West Sleekburn Welfare. Bebside Gordon. Blyth Spartans May 1925. Bebside Gordon January 1926. Bedlington United (trial) August 1926. Stakeford United September 1926. Bebside Gordon July 1927. ASHINGTON amateur (trial) August 1927. Bebside Gordon. Heart of Midlothian (trial) October 1927. ASHINGTON professional May 1928. Seaton Delaval December 1929. Bedlington United August 1930. Blyth Spartans June 1931. Hexham cs 1936. West Sleekburn Welfare Committee by 1948.
Debut v Barrow (h) 29.9.28, won 1-0
Elder brother of Joe, a centre-forward with Frickley Colliery and Carlisle United. Tom was signed in May 1928 following trials at Portland Park in August 1927 and with Heart of Midlothian in October of the same year. At just 21 years of age the strapping wing-half was a terrier-like tackler, his great strength enabling him to finish a game as fresh as when he started it. His first team involvement began in promising fashion, three wins accruing from his first five matches, but his initial run of seven matches also included heavy defeats at home to Bradford City (2-8) and away at Carlisle United (1-5). A return to reserve team football followed, but with the first team in freefall and without a win in six matches he was reintroduced but was unable to stem the tide of defeat, his return on February 16th featured eleven goals at Portland Park, Doncaster Rovers winning 7-4, six goals being scored by Tom Keetley, Rovers' centre-forward.
Appearances: FL: 17 apps 0 gls Total: 17 apps 0 gls

CHESTER, Charles 'Carlyle'

Right-half
5' 8"   10st 6lbs
Born: Barton Irwell, 5 September 1903
Died: Ulverston, 13 October 1969
Career: Northumberland County. Luton Town 1924. ASHINGTON amateur May 1925. Ulverston Town July 1929.
Debut v New Brighton (a) 5.9.25, drawn 1-1
As an amateur, Carlyle Chester won his county cap, but he was unable to break into Luton Town's Third Division South side. Sparingly used during his first season at Portland Park while being nursed in the reserve side, he was afforded more opportunities in 1926-27, but was never at his best on heavy grounds, his lack of physical advantage exposed in such conditions.
Appearances: FL: 15 apps 0 gls FAC: 3 apps 0 gls Total: 18 apps 0 gls

CHIPPERFIELD, Francis "Frank"

Left-half
5' 11"   11st 12lbs
Born: Shiremoor, Newcastle-on-Tyne, 2 December 1895
Died: Shiremoor, Newcastle-on-Tyne, 8 March 1979
Career: Bates United. South Shields (trial). Blyth Spartans. Leeds City 1918-19, fee £250. Lincoln City October 1919, fee £100. Middlesbrough June 1920, fee £800. Blyth Spartans (loan) June 1921. Carlisle United (loan) June 1922. ASHINGTON June 1923. Frickley Colliery June 1929.
Debut v Wrexham (a) 25.8.23, lost 0-4
The demise of the Leeds City club – formally closed down by the FA for financial irregularities – led to a unique auction of the club's players at the Metropole Hotel in

Leeds on 17th October 1919. Frank Chipperfield was one of the players to go under the auctioneer's hammer, and he proved a great bargain at £100, as Lincoln City sold him, less than a year later, to Middlesbrough for a very handsome profit. He played in only one First Division match – a 6-2 defeat at Wolverhampton Wanderers in October 1920 – and was loaned to Blyth Spartans for the 1920-21 season. In a similar arrangement, he was loaned to Carlisle United for 1922-23, but when released on a free transfer at the end of the season he was quickly snapped up by Ashington. The tall, fair-haired wing-half, who had served in the RGA during the First World War, must rank as one of the best free transfer signings made by the Colliers. A strong defensive game, coupled with good headwork and a useful left foot shot ranked him amongst the best wing-halves operating in the Northern Section.
Appearances: FL: 164 apps 9 gls FAC: 9 apps 0 gls Total: 173 apps 9 gls

CLARK, Hector

Outside-right
Born: Morpeth, 8 December 1904
Died: Morpeth, 29 July 1983
Career: ASHINGTON amateur May 1928, registered for FL matches September 1928.
Debut v New Brighton (a) 8.9.28, lost 2-3
Hector Clark's debut in League football was made in atrocious weather, incessant rain restricting the attendance at Rake Lane to 3,244 spectators. Despite winning the toss and taking advantage of the slope, New Brighton found themselves two goals down at the interval, George Johnson scoring in the 13th and 35th minutes. Within a quarter of an hour of the restart, New Brighton were level, and twenty minutes from time they scored the winner. Clark had struggled to make headway on the right wing, faced by New Brighton's Len Carr, one of the Northern Section's best defenders, with in excess of 300 League appearances for the Rakers.
Appearances: FL: 2 apps 0 gls Total: 2 apps 0 gls

CLARK, James Robinson

Inside-left
5' 8"   10st 7lbs
Born: Bensham, Gateshead, 20 October 1895
Died: Gateshead, 16 September 1947
Career: Annfield Plain. Jarrow. Newcastle United December 1921, fee £300. Leeds United May 1924, fee £300. Swindon Town June 1925. Greenock Morton December 1926. ASHINGTON March-May 1927. Shelbourne 1928.
Debut v Accrington Stanley (a) 19.3.27, lost 0-3
In two and a half seasons with Newcastle United, Jimmy Clark found few senior opportunities (11 appearances and two goals), despite his outstanding record in the North-Eastern League side. His total of 46 goals for the reserves included 20 in 1922-23 when the league title was won, he was also second highest scorer in 1921-22 and 1923-24. His best subsequent spell was with Swindon Town (18 appearances and seven goals), this followed a disappointing season with Leeds United (three appearances and no goals). He played only once in Scottish League football before joining the Colliers in the closing months of season 1927 28. His brief stay ended painfully as he was injured and carried from the field, early in the second half of the crushing 6-2 defeat at Stockport County in the penultimate fixture of the campaign. Clark's football career wound up in Irish football and he later returned to Tyneside, where he worked at the Wright-Anderson steelworks. He died, aged 51, from tuberculosis.
Appearances: FL: 5 apps 0 gls Total: 5 apps 0 gls

COLLIER, James

Left-half   5' 10½" 11st 5lbs
Born: Seaton Delaval, 3 April 1897
Died: Seaton Delaval, January quarter 1980
Career: Blyth Spartans. Burnley (trial) April 1920. Crystal Palace May 1920. ASHINGTON August 1922 to cs 1923.
Debut v Wigan Borough (h) 2.9.22, won 2-1
Despite association with Burnley and Crystal Palace, Collier lacked League experience, having played just once for Palace before sustaining a broken leg during their Third Division championship season, 1920-21. Although fully recovered for the start of the following season, he did not feature in the first team again. After appearing in eleven consecutive matches at the start of the season, when a fairly settled line-up gave the Colliers a promising start, he lost his place, reappearing in late season at left full-back, as deputy for long-serving stalwart, George Hamilton.
Appearances: FL: 17 apps 0 gls FAC: 1 app 0 gls Total: 18 apps 0 gls

COOMBS, Joseph

Right-half   5' 8"   11st 2lbs
Born: Ashington, 2 March 1902
Died: Ashington, July quarter 1971
Career: Ashington Welfare amateur August 1926. ASHINGTON trial August 1926, amateur November 1927, professional May 1928. Wallaw United January 1931. Pegswood United August 1932.
Debut v New Brighton (h) 7.1.28, won 3-2
Introduced at right-half in mid season 1927-28, local amateur Joe Coombs' Football League career was off to a good start, a sequence of four matches without a victory being broken in the home match against New Brighton. The outcome of three goals to two in Ashington's favour was not a true reflection of the play, but they recovered from being 2-1 in arrears. Injury to New Brighton's centre-half, Jack Reid, left them with ten men for most of the second half, and the Colliers were quick to take advantage. While still in the unpaid ranks Coombs enjoyed a run of eighteen consecutive matches, alongside seasoned campaigners Jimmy Price and Francis Chipperfield in the middle line. At the commencement of the 1928-29 season, two players initially blocked his path. Arthur Dalkin and Tom Thirwell, who were both embarking on a second spell at Portland Park, began the season in the wing-half berths. Further competition arrived when Tom Wilson was signed in November, restricting Joe Coombs to just eight appearances in his final season.
Appearances: FL: 26 apps 0 gls FAC: 1 app 0 gls Total: 27 apps 0 gls

COOPER, John William

Outside-right   5' 8½"   11st 0lbs
Born: Bebside, Northumberland, July quarter 1906
Career: Bebside Gordon. Blyth Spartans. ASHINGTON amateur October 1924. Bebside Gordon. Blyth Spartans. New Delaval Villa August 1927. Bebside Gordon February 1929.
Debut v Accrington Stanley (h) 25.10.24, lost 1-2
A lack of firepower in attack in the early months of season 1924-25 led to numerous team changes, with the outside-right position a particular problem throughout, eight different players occupying the berth during the season. After two consecutive outings, the youthful former Blyth Spartans wingman Cooper was said to have found little opportunity to show his ability on the ball. In both matches the team were heavily criticised, the defenders indulging in too much hefty kicking – the ball being continually in the air when ground passes would have been more advantageous. The halves were said to be indifferent and the forward line disjointed. At least a share of the points resulted in Cooper's second and final outing, a goal-less draw at Halifax Town.
Appearances: FL: 2 apps 0 gls Total: 2 apps 0 gls

COUSINS, Harry Douglas

Inside-right
5' 8"   10st 10lbs
Born: Coundon Grange, Bishop Auckland, 6 December 1897
Died: Eastbourne, 21 April 1978
Career: Tanfield Lea Institute. West Stanley August 1919. Annfield Plain. Durham City August 1920. Stockport County May 1922. Southport June 1923. Bangor City October 1925. ASHINGTON December 1925, fee £150. Nelson (trial) September-November 1926. Stalybridge Celtic November 1926 to February 1927.
Debut v Barrow (h) 25.12.25, lost 1-4 (scored)
Harry Cousins became the first Durham City player to score a hat-trick in a Football League match, this coming against Crewe Alexandra in a 4-2 victory at Kepier Haughs in January 1922. His 17 goals during the season saw him head the scoring list. He did less well in a season with Stockport County, scoring three goals in 14 matches. Two seasons with Southport followed in which he netted 13 goals in 44 matches, but a personal highlight came in a reserve team match against Wigan Borough Reserves in February 1925 when he scored six goals in a 7-3 win. In terms of League football, his sojourn with the Colliers proved to be his swansong in senior football. For many years he ran a credit drapery business in Southport, later moving to Eastbourne where, at the age of 81, he fell out of bed and broke his neck, tragically leaving him paralysed. Within a matter of weeks he died. It was a sad and bizarre ending to a long life that had been spent mainly in excellent health and spirits.
Appearances: FL: 8 apps 3 gls Total: 8 apps 3 gls

COUTTS, Thomas

Wing-half   5' 8½"   11st 4lbs
Born: Birtley, 10 May 1902
Died: Botley, Hants, 26 December 1968
Career: Saltwell Villa. ASHINGTON November 1923. Dunston Atlas Villa cs 1926. Leeds United January 1927. Southampton June 1928. Newport (Isle of Wight) November 1929 to 1939.
Debut v Rochdale (a) 19.1.24, lost 0-1
Arriving from Saltwell Villa in November 1923, Tom Coutts took some time to adjust to the pace of senior football, but had shown sufficient progress to earn an extended run of 27 consecutive League matches in his first full season when the Colliers recovered from an indifferent start to reach tenth place in the final table. After a brief spell in non-League football he joined Leeds United but made only one League appearance in their Division Two promotion season. His spell with Southampton was spent entirely in reserve ranks, but he enjoyed a lengthy association with Newport (Isle of Wight) before the outbreak of World War Two enforced his retirement at the age of 37.
Appearances: FL: 46 apps 0 gls Total: 46 apps 0 gls

CRAIG, Thomas

Centre-forward   5' 7"   11st 0lbs
Born: Tullibody, near Stirling.
Career: Rowlands Gill. Welbeck Athletic. ASHINGTON amateur April 1926.
Debut v Chesterfield (a) 1.5.26, lost 1-6
Said to have scored 79 goals for Welbeck Athletic in season 1925-26, bustling centre-forward Tom Craig found the step up to senior football a far from rewarding experience. The Colliers sustained their heaviest defeat of the season on his debut, the local correspondent considering: "Ashington did not discover the right class of centre-forward in Craig."
Appearances: FL: 1 app 0 gls Total: 1 app 0 gls

CRANE, John Pringle

Left-half
Born: Newcastle-on-Tyne, 23 December 1903
Died: Tynemouth, 2 January 1990
Career: Jesmond Villa. Durham University. Durham County Amateurs. Wallsend February 1924. Bede College. ASHINGTON amateur August 1925. Annfield Plain April 1926 to 1932. Jarrow cs 1935.
Debut v Wigan Borough (h) 29.8.25, drawn 3-3
With a rather curious turn of phrase, the *Newcastle Journal's* correspondent considered: "On his Football League debut J.P. Crane was rather gentle against a robust side". From which we might assume that he failed to "get stuck in" against vigorous opponents who won a share of the points after trailing 3-1 after 28 minutes play. The County amateur had won his chance in the League side after impressing in the final trial match, the accuracy of his passing being particularly notable. The fact that he did not get a second senior outing led to his move to Annfield Plain, and he went on to enjoy a lengthy and successful association with them, joining during the season that they gained admission to the North Eastern League (on their fifth application), having previously been members of the Northern Alliance.
Appearances: FL: 1 app 0 gls Total: 1 app 0 gls

DALKIN, Arthur Ernest

Right-half   5' 11"   11st 12lbs
Born: Ashington, 6 March 1906
Died: Ashington, January 1990
Career: Benfieldside Schoolboys. Ashington Colliery Welfare 1924-25. Bedlington United. ASHINGTON amateur March 1926. Preston Colliery June 1927. ASHINGTON July 1928. Frickley Colliery September 1929. South Kirkby Colliery February 1930.
Debut v Bradford Park Avenue (h) 26.2.27, drawn 2-2
The younger brother of Joseph William (q.v.), Arthur represented the Derwent Valley League as a youngster. He signed an amateur form with the Colliers in March 1926 and appeared in nine first team matches before joining Preston Colliery, along with his brother, in June 1927. Both returned to Portland Park for a second spell in August 1928, and the pair first appeared together in a Football League match at New Brighton on 8th September. They were unable to mark the occasion with a victory, but they did collect a winning bonus three weeks later in a 1-0 victory against Barrow at Portland Park. During the relegation season, Arthur made 26 League appearances, proving a sound and reliable wing-half with a useful dash of versatility.
Appearances: FL: 35 apps 0 gls FAC: 1 app 0 gls Total: 36 apps 0 gls

DALKIN, Joseph William

Outside-right
5' 8"   11st 5lbs
Born: Ashington, 10 February 1901
Career: Bedlington United. ASHINGTON June 1925. Preston Colliery June 1927. ASHINGTON August 1928. Walker Celtic August 1930. Bedlington United September 1932. Pegswood United December 1933. Wallaw United. Bedlington District Pit Welfare September 1936.
Debut v Barrow (a) 1.1.26, won 3-2 (scored one)
A highly successful mid season switch brought immediate dividends, when Billy Turnbull was moved from outside-right to centre-forward, with Joe Dalkin taking over on the right wing. The newcomer scored the winner on his debut in the Football League and had scored five goals within the space of just seven first team outings. Turnbull, meanwhile, notched three hat-tricks and 14 goals in 13 matches as attack leader, leading to his upward move to Manchester City. Six goals in 20 appearances spanning the second half of the 1925-26 season was the highlight of Joe Dalkin's career, as he did little of note in the following season (12 appearances and one goal). He was in and out of the first team in his final season of League action, having returned to Portland Park after a season spent with Preston Colliery.
Appearances: FL: 46 apps 7 gls Total: 46 apps 7 gls

DARGUE, Thomas Johnson

Inside-left
Born: Morpeth, 11 August 1893
Died: Morpeth, October quarter 1951
Career: Stakeford United. ASHINGTON November 1921. Stakeford United October 1922. Guide Post United October 1926.
Debut v Lincoln City (h) 12.11.21, won 4-2 (scored one)
The Colliers fielded two new inside forwards and brought Alex Davidson back into goal for the return fixture with Lincoln City in November 1921. Both of the new forwards, Dargue and Galloway, netted in the 4-2 victory, the inclusion of the newcomers bringing a great improvement to the forward line. In bright sunshine Ashington were ahead after just three minutes play, Knowles netting from a well placed corner by Thompson. Lincoln quickly equalised, but Galloway restored the lead, only for Boylen to bring the scores level again. In the second half, the Colliers dominated, with Robertson and Dargue scoring within three minutes of one another. Tom Dargue was said to need a little more experience, but the local correspondent noted that he certainly knew where the goals were. Certainly, his strike rate was an impressive one during his relatively brief career in senior football.
Appearances: FL: 15 apps 8 gls FAC: 3 apps 2 gls Total: 18 apps 10 gls

DAVIDSON, Alexander Godwin

Goalkeeper   5' 7½"   11st 2lbs
Born: Newcastle-on-Tyne, 22 September 1899
Career: Close Works (Gateshead). ASHINGTON August 1920. Annfield Plain November 1925.
Debut v Grimsby Town (h) 27.8.21, won 1-0
Although on the short side for his position, Alex Davidson was strongly built and well able to withstand the buffeting that was a part of the goalkeeper's lot in early days, when both ball and goalkeeper could finish up in the net, and all quite legitimately. Davidson was also possessed of keen anticipation, a quick eye, and was extremely reliable. Quick reflexes made him a difficult man to beat from the penalty spot, as instanced by his saves against Chesterfield and Hartlepools United in 1921-22, Walsall in 1922-23 and Doncaster Rovers in 1923-24. He was reported to have joined Workington in June 1923, but he continued with Ashington in August and September of the same year, with a final two appearances spanning March and April 1924.
Appearances: FL: 42 apps 0 gls FAC: 4 apps 0 gls Total: 46 apps 0 gls

DAVIDSON, Nicholas Tiesdell

Inside-left   5' 7"   10st 7lbs
Born: Wallsend-on-Tyne, April quarter 1901
Died: Wallsend-on-Tyne, October qurter 1956
Career: Backworth United. Blyth Spartans October 1919. Middlesbrough April 1920. ASHINGTON October 1922. Carlisle United March 1923. Mold Town July 1924. Caernarfon Town July 1926. Washington Colliery Welfare August 1927. Wallsend August 1929.
Debut v Chesterfield (a) 21.10.22, drawn 2-2
A perceived weakness at inside-left led to the signing of Nichol Davidson, a 21 year-old with experience in Middlesborough's reserve ranks. The lightly built forward was somewhat handicapped by lack of inches but controlled the ball well and impressed in approach work. Said to be in need of a little more steadiness in front of goal, he netted in his second appearance, a 2-0 home win against Chesterfield, but failed to score thereafter. The Colliers shortcomings in attack persisted throughout the season that ended with a 19th place finish and a re-election application.
Appearances: FL: 13 apps 1 gl Total: 13 apps 1 gl

DAVISON, James Hood

Inside-right   5' 10"   10st 8lbs
Born: Ashington, 5 December 1905
Died: Ashington, February 1991
Career: Ashington Colliery Welfare. ASHINGTON June 1924. Ashington Colliery Welfare. ASHINGTON again as an amateur September 1928.
Debut v Chesterfield (a) 22.9.28, lost 1 – 4
The opening practice match at Portland Park in August 1928 attracted a gate of 2,000 spectators, and the "Whites" won 6-1 in a keen encounter. Leslie Campbell, a product from Lintz Colliery, showed fine marksmanship in scoring a "hat trick", and later signed an amateur form but did not get an opportunity in the League side. Davison, ex Ashington Colliery Welfare, was said to be the only player in the "Stripes" forward line to show initiation. He did manage to make a Football League appearance, but his solitary outing failed to have the desired effect as the Colliers lost their fifth consecutive away match. The fact that they won only twice on their travels during the season contributed largely to their occupation of the last place in the league table and subsequent loss of Football League status. On Davison's debut, Chesterfield were said to have played a robust game, and Ashington were kept largely on the defensive, although they pressed strongly in the early stages, when centre-forward George Johnson twice failed with the goal at his mercy. Randall's goal for the Colliers was due reward for brilliant opportunism, but it came only as a late consolation in the 4-1 defeat.
Appearances: FL: 1 app 0 gls Total: 1 app 0 gls

DICKINSON, Joseph Henry

Inside-right   5' 7"   11st 3lbs
Born: Choppington, October quarter 1900
Died: Choppington, April quarter 1950
Career: Choppington. Hartlepools United (trial) June 1919. Choppington. South Shields (trial) August 1919. Choppington. Sunderland March 1921. ASHINGTON July 1921. Bedlington United cs 1922. Amble September 1927.
Debut v Grimsby Town (h) 27.8.21, won 1-0 (scored)
The scorer of Ashington's first goal in the Football League, Joe Dickinson's trio of senior appearances with the Colliers was his only taste of League football, despite his association with three other League clubs. His historic goal came in the second half of a bruising encounter. When Moody, Grimsby Town's goalkeeper, fisted out a centre from Joe Brayson, the ball landed at the feet of Dickinson who gently lobbed the ball back into goal, his success being recognised by "tremendous cheers" according to the local correspondent. His afternoon was spoilt shortly afterwards when he was knocked senseless and had to retire.
Appearances: FL: 3 apps 1 gl Total: 3 apps 1 gl

DIXON, Andrew Gilfilling

Goalkeeper   5' 9"   10st 4lbs
Born: Ashington, 23 May 1905
Died: Ashington, April 1987
Career: Ashington Welfare. ASHINGTON amateur August 1928. Ashington Welfare October 1928.
Debut v Darlington (h) 27.8.28, won 4-2
When former Newcastle United goalkeeper Bradley was injured in the season's opening fixture at Southport he was not sufficiently recovered to turn out, just two days later, against Darlington at Portland Park. Happily, the side was in no way weakened by the inclusion of Dixon, who gave a fine display in goal. The Colliers led 3-1 at the interval and were indebted to their young goalkeeper who fielded hard drives by Moloney, McQuire and Dickson in the second half, eventually being beaten when Colliers full-back Richardson headed through his own goal. Ashington claimed the points in a 4-2 victory, their best result at Portland Park in a depressing season that ended with an unsuccessful re-election application.
Appearances: FL: 1 app 0 gls Total: 1 app 0 gls

DRAPER, John Percy

Centre-forward
Born: Lanchester, 18 June 1901
Died: Sunderland, April quarter 1978
Career: Usworth Colliery. Middlesbrough amateur. ASHINGTON January 1923.
Debut v Wrexham (h) 20.1.23, drawn 1-1
John Draper followed Nichol Davidson to Portland Park, both forwards with experience in the reserve ranks of Middlesbrough. Draper's brief taste of League football did not lack variety. Draws against Wrexham, at home and away, were followed by a defeat at Crewe and a home win against Grimsby Town. In what proved to be his final outing, a 4-7 defeat at Grimsby Town, the match featured four goals by Jimmy Carmichael, the Mariner's start centre-forward. It was only the second time that the Colliers' had recorded four goals in a match during that season, but on this occasion, two of the goals were own goals by Grimsby defenders.
Appearances: FL: 5 apps 1 gl Total: 5 apps 1 gl

ELLIOTT, John William

Goalkeeper
5' 11½" 13st 2lbs
Born: Wallsend, 24 May 1898
Died: Newcastle-on-Tyne, April quarter 1969
Career: Scotswood. Preston North End February 1921. Watford cs 1923 to February 1924. Scotswood July 1924. Jarrow. ASHINGTON June 1925. Scotswood October 1927. Jarrow July 1928. Walker Park 1929. Scotswood August 1930. Newcastle Tramways October 1934.
Debut v Wigan Borough (h) 29.8.25, drawn 3-3
The *Lancashire Post Annual* for 1921-22 considered that Elliott's cool and discerning work between the posts was in some ways reminiscent of the style of Peter McBride, which was high praise indeed. McBride, capped on six occasions by Scotland had guarded North End's goal between 1897-1912, clocking up 442 Football League appearances. Recruited by North End from North Eastern League football in February 1921, Elliott played so well that he earned a place in the first team, shortly before the end of the season, in a 2-2 draw at Sunderland on April 23rd. He began the following season as first choice but was dropped after seven matches, in a season when five different goalkeepers were fielded. North End reached the final of the FA Cup but lost 1-0 to Huddersfield Town. Mitchell maintaining his position in goal throughout the cup-ties. Without a senior appearance for Watford, Elliott resumed his League career with Ashington. Despite playing with the handicap of deafness – caused by an accident while playing in junior football before joining

Preston North End – his 57 first team appearances for the Colliers were made consecutively, but the team's indifferent start to season 1926-27 saw him replaced by Ralph Ridley, who held on to the first team jersey from mid November until the end of the season.

Appearances: FL: 56 apps 0 gls FAC: 1 app 0 gls Total: 57 apps 0 gls

ELSDON, William Rowell

Outside-left
Born: Hexham, 19 April 1900
Died: Newcastle-on-Tyne, 24 February 1984
Career: ASHINGTON amateur December 1928.
Debut v Nelson (h) 1.1.29, won 3-2

New Years Day 1929 marked the solitary League appearance of amateur wingman W.R. Elsdon, and the 3-2 victory over mid-table Nelson was a welcome relief to the 1,344 spectators at Portland Park. The Colliers ended a two-month run of eleven matches without a victory thanks to a hat-trick scored by centre-forward J.W. Robson. Sadly, a further two months had elapsed before the side won another match, on this occasion a hat-trick scored by George Johnson accounted for Hartlepools United in a rare 3-1 away success. At the season's close, both Hartlepools and Ashington were obliged to apply for re-election, but it was the Colliers who were the unsuccessful applicants.

Appearances: FL: 1 app 0 gls Total: 1 app 0 gls

FEATHERSTONE, Henry Wilson "Harry"

Full-back   5' 9"   12st 2lbs
Born: Wallsend, 20 June 1888
Died: Bill Quay, Northumberland, 23 February 1956
Career: Wallsend Park Villa. St. Mirren May 1909. Cardiff City cs 1911. Ashington United June1914. Linfield October 1918. Belfast United September 1920. ASHINGTON November 1920. Halifax Town August 1923. Victoria Garesfield January 1925. Stanley United *circa* 1926.
Debut v Grimsby Town (h) 27.8.21, won 1-0

Harry Featherstone began in senior football with St Mirren, when he was one of a pair of full-backs, along with Harry Harvey, recruited from Wallsend Park Villa in May 1909. In two seasons at Love Street Featherstone made 37 Scottish League appearances and scored six goals, having switched from full-back to centre-forward in season 1910-11. He made an immediate impact following his transfer to Cardiff City, scoring four goals in a 5-1 win against Cwm

Albion in his third Southern League appearance, and 16 goals in all matches, including one in the Welsh Cup Final replay, a 3-0 victory against Pontypridd. In 1912-13 he scored four goals in ten Southern League matches, Cardiff winning the championship of the Second Division, losing only one league match during the successful season. His wandering path continued, two separate spells in Irish football preceding his arrival at Portland Park in November 1920, the Colliers' last season in the North Eastern League, prior to their election into the Northern Section of the Third Division for season 1921-22. Having by this time reverted to defensive duties, his two seasons of League action found him generally at full-back, but he also occupied both flanks at wing-half when required. His three goals all came from successful penalty conversions, one such against Nelson in January 1922 was only awarded after lengthy consultation between referee and linesman as the markings of the penalty area had been obscured by snow that blanketed the ground throughout the match. A goal from the penalty spot marked his August 1923 debut with Halifax Town, in a 1-1 draw at Lincoln City, and he scored at the second attempt against New Brighton in the following month, after the Rakers' goalkeeper Mehaffy had saved his first spot kick. Ironically, after appearing in the first thirteen League matches, Featherstone lost his first team place following Halifax's 4-0 defeat at Ashington on November 3rd, reappearing in late season for a further seven outings, his last in senior football.

Appearances: FL: 66 apps 3 gls FAC: 5 apps 0 gls 71 apps 3 gls

Honours: Cardiff City: Welsh Cup winners 1912. Southern League Division Two champions 1913. Linfield: Irish Cup and Charity Cup winners in 1919. Represented England v Ireland in a charity match in 1918.

FENWICK, Alfred Randolph

Centre-half
5' 11"   12st 2lbs
Born: Hamsterley,
26 March 1891
Died: Hamsterley,
22 March 1975
Career: Craghead
United. Hull City
October 1911. West
Ham United April
1914. Wartime
guest player with
Hartlepools United and South Shields. Coventry City December 1919. Craghead United August 1921. Blyth Spartans August 1922. ASHINGTON May 1924. Blyth Spartans December 1924. Bedlington United August 1926. Blyth Spartans coach February 1929, then a director to November 1946.
Debut v Chesterfield (h) 30.8.24, won 2-1
Two of Fenwick's football playing relations included cousin Austin Campbell, the English international wing half, while a son, also named Alfred, was a reserve full-back with Sheffield Wednesday and Reading in the late 1930s. Alf senior began in Division Two with Hull City as a wing half, but shone as an emergency centre-forward scoring five goals in four matches in April 1913. He found few opportunities after moving to West Ham United, but was pitched straight into Coventry City's battle to retain Second Division status. When Fenwick made his debut at home to Clapton Orient on 20th December 1919, his new team were without a win in eighteen matches, but he was able to assist them to turn the tide. Nine wins in the second half of the season took them to safety in 20th position. After another season of similar struggles and a 21st place finish, Fenwick returned to his first club, Craghead United, subsequently spending half of a season with the Colliers before returning to non-League circles at the age of 34. Two wins and a draw in the first three matches was a promising start for the Colliers in 1924-25, but when Alf Fenwick played in his last League match, a 1-2 defeat by Accrington Stanley on 25th October, their record was less impressive – 9 points taken from 13 matches, 14 goals scored and 28 conceded. Within the sequence, the veteran defender had become

the first Ashington player to be sent off the field in a Football League match, his dismissal coming on the hour in the 5-2 home win against Barrow on 13th September 1924.
Appearances: FL: 12 apps 0 gls Total: 12 apps 0 gls

FERGUSON, Edward "Ted"

Right-back
5' 9"   12st 7lbs
Born: Seaton Burn, 2 August 1895
Died: Seaton Burn, 8 February 1978
Career: Seaton Burn. Army football. ASHINGTON June 1919. Chelsea March 1920. ASHINGTON June 1924.
Nelson August 1928. Annfield Plain August 1930. Seaton Burn Welfare amateur July 1933.
Debut v Chesterfield (h) 30.8.24, won 2-1
A robust and quick tackling defender, Ted Ferguson hailed from a family of footballers. Brothers included Robert (West Bromwich Albion and Nelson), William (Annfield Plain) and a nephew, Cecil Ferguson (Newcastle United). Ted Ferguson began with Ashington in North Eastern League days, and before the end of his first season, he gained an upward move to Chelsea, but in four plus years he failed to break into the league side, making just two first team appearances. A return to Portland Park saw his old club by this time operating in the Northern Section of Division Three. In his third season an injury sustained at Nottingham Forest in a third round FA Cup-tie on January 8th brought his season to a premature end, and he did not play regular first team football for almost a year. Joining Nelson in late August 1928 he was quickly installed at right full-back and played a large part in the improved defensive qualities of a team that had conceded a staggering 136

goals in League matches in the season prior to his arrival.
Appearances: FL: 119 apps 5 gls FAC: 6 apps 0 gls Total: 125 apps 5 gls

FOSTER, John Thomas "Jackie"

Winger
5' 6½"   10st 10lbs
Born: Southwick, Sunderland, 21 March 1902
Career: Southwick Central School. Sunderland Schoolboys. Wearmouth Colliery School 1915. Durham County Schoolboys 1915-16. Hylton Colliery Juniors 1917. Murton Athletic 1919. Sunderland August 1920. ASHINGTON June 1921. Halifax Town September 1923. Grimsby Town May 1925. Bristol City June 1926. Brentford May 1929. Barrow July 1933 to June 1936. Colwyn Bay United player-coach October 1936. Ashford Town (trial) September-November 1937. Brentford ground staff cs 1938. Royal Racing Club, Belgium, coach 1946.
Debut v Grimsby Town (h) 27.8.21, won 1-0
Jackie Foster was associated with three Third Division championship sides (Grimsby Town 1926, Bristol City 1927 and Brentford 1933)

but qualified for a medal only with the latter. At that period the Bees were a high-flying Southern Section outfit who, after nudging promotion for three years, finally made it, going on to the top flight two seasons later. Foster enjoyed sixteen years of League fare, his best run coming late with Brentford (141 League appearances). Speedy runs and quick transfers were features of Foster's play, and he was particularly effective in his second season with the Colliers, being one of a pair of players (Tom Robertson the other) who appeared in every League and Cup match during the season. Barrow was his last port of call in senior football, in three seasons he netted 22 goals in 94 matches, later returning to the town to take over the management of the Regal Bar in Forshaw Street.

Appearances: FL: 68 apps 5 gls FAC: 2 apps 1 gl Total: 70 apps 6 gls
Honours: Brentford: Division Three South champions 1933.

GAFFNEY, Peter

Centre-half   6' 0"   12st 6lbs
Born: Kirknewton, 9 November 1897
Career: Loanhead Mayflower. Bo'ness February 1920. Hamilton Academical 1919-20. Alloa Athletic May 1921. Dunfermline Athletic October 1922. Doncaster Rovers June 1923, fee £50. Denaby United February 1924. Barrow June 1924. New Brighton April 1925. Coventry City June 1926. ASHINGTON (trial) August 1927. Torquay United September 1927. Aldershot November 1927.
Debut v Halifax Town (a) 5.9.27, lost 1-6

A promotion winner with Alloa Athletic in season 1921-22, Peter Gaffney did less well after crossing the border, initially to join Doncaster Rovers in June 1923. His best spell in English football came with New Brighton for whom he scored three goals in 19 League appearances, his debut being made against Ashington on 5th September 1925. By training a centre-half, he nevertheless had an extended run at centre-forward following the Rakers sale of Jimmy Dunne to Sheffield United. He arrived at Portland Park, on trial, after leaving Coventry City, in time to feature in the third pre-season practice match. Appearing in the "Possibles" team, who were beaten 4-2 by the "Probables", he was said to have played well up to a point, but was short of match fitness. The fact that his single League appearance resulted in a 6-1 defeat at Halifax Town, led to his departure later in the same month, having failed to win an extension to his one-month trial.

Appearances: FL: 1 app 0 gls Total: 1 app 0 gls

GALLOWAY, William Walton

Inside-right
5' 7"   9st 12lbs
Born: Newcastle-on-Tyne, 13 November 1894
Died: Gateshead, April quarter 1969
Career: Northumberland County Schoolboys. Army football with the 19th Northumberland Fusiliers from 1914.

Later during WW1 commissioned in the Air Force during which time he represented the Egyptian Expeditionary Force. Post-war with Newcastle Bohemians and Northumberland County Amateurs. ASHINGTON amateur November 1921.
Debut v Lincoln City (h) 12.11.21, won 4-2 (scored one)

Following a match in the Northumberland Amateur County Championship attended by the Ashington club's Directors, William Galloway was induced to sign an amateur form, with a view to strengthening their underachieving forward line. The newcomer did not disappoint, as he scored in each of his first two outings in League football. His favourite position was on the extreme right, but he was fielded at inside-right and centre-forward, prompting one correspondent to write: "Put Galloway into his proper position (outside-right) and he is an International." Certainly he was among the forefront of the many amateur players who wore the Colliers' colours in League action, and he made a valuable contribution in helping the team to finish in tenth position in their first season in the Football League. Shortly after the *Topical Times* reported that Tottenham Hotspur

were showing an interest, Galloway's season was cruelly cut short, following an injury sustained at Southport on March 11th.
Appearances: FL: 11 apps 6 gls FAC: 3 apps 0 gls Total: 14 apps 6 gls

GARDNER, William

Inside-right
5' 7½"   12st 6lbs
Born: Langley Moor, 7 June 1893
Died: Meadowfield, County Durham, 9 February 1973
Career: St Helen's School (Auckland). Redworth. St Helen's United. Brandon Institute. St Helen's W.M. Club. Durham City. Crook Town. Bishop Auckland *circa* 1913. Derby County August 1920. Stockport County August 1921. Spennymoor United November 1921. Queens Park Rangers March 1923. ASHINGTON July 1923. Grimsby Town October 1925, fee £500. Darlington September 1927. Torquay United June 1928. York City July 1929. Crewe Alexandra July 1931. Rochdale September 1932, retired in 1933.
Debut v Wrexham (a) 25.8.23, lost 0-4
Bill Gardner made League appearances for nine different clubs after starring in amateur ranks with Bishop Auckland. In season 1919-20 he scored 56 goals for his club and five for England Amateurs, including four against Wales at Merthyr. The short but weighty inside-forward commenced his professional career with Derby County, but it was not until he reached Ashington that his career took off. Leading scorer in both of his full seasons at Portland Park, he brought a useful fee to the Colliers' coffers when transferred to Grimsby Town. He passed the milestone of 200 League appearances in the colours of York City and made his 214th and final appearance with Rochdale at the age of 39, having scored a career total of 95 League goals.
Appearances: FL: 84 apps 38 gls FAC: 6 apps 5 gls Total: 90 apps 43 gls
Honours: England Amateur International versus Wales and Belgium in 1920.

Bishop Auckland: FA Amateur Cup finalists 1915.
Represented the North Eastern League v the Central League at Newcastle in February 1923 and scored a hat-trick in the 4-1 win.

GOONAN, Michael

Outside-left   5' 6"   10st 2lbs
Born: Gosforth, Newcastle-on-Tyne, 17 April 1899
Died: Bedlington, 15 March 1991
Career: West Sleekburn. ASHINGTON June 1922. Bedlington United August 1923. Seaton Delaval March 1924. Stakeford United July 1926. Cramlington Rovers October 1926. Stakeford United January 1927. Blyth Spartans October 1927. Bedlington United. Blyth Spartans January 1928. Bedlington United October 1930.
Debut v Chesterfield (a) 21.10.22, drawn 2-2
Michael Goonan impressed in pre-season trials at Portland Park, his "nippy work" being praised in the "Reds" 5-3 victory against the "Stripes" in mid August 1922. The lightweight wingman was, however, selected only once for League action as deputy for Tom McCloud and he failed to retain his position on the left flank. Tommy Robson being brought in for his solitary League outing for the return match against Chesterfield before McCloud's return to fitness and first team action.
Appearances: FL: 1 app 0 gls Total: 1 app 0 gls

GRAHAM, Ernest

Inside-right
Born: New Delaval, July quarter 1906
Career: New Delaval Villa. Dundee (trial) December 1926. ASHINGTON amateur August 1927. Blyth Spartans August 1928. ASHINGTON August 1929. New Delaval Villa November 1929.
Debut v Wrexham (a) 5.11.27, lost 1-5
Signed on amateur forms with a view to assisting the reserve team, Graham was introduced to League action as one of two changes made for the trip to Wrexham. Graham was introduced at centre-forward with J.F. Noble taking the inside-right berth. Terrible conditions prevailed at Wrexham with half a gale blowing while rain fell

heavily throughout. Struggling against the fierce wind in the first half, the Colliers were three goals down at the interval. The second half was more even, but Cecil Smith the Welshmen's centre-forward completed his hat-trick while Rogers scored the other two goals, Randall netting for the Colliers. Despite his difficult introduction to League football, Graham retained his place in the side but was switched to inside-right where, despite a lack of composure when, according to the local correspondent, missing "golden opportunities", he nevertheless netted half a dozen valuable goals as the side successfully avoided the need of a re-election application.
Appearances: FL: 14 apps 6 gls FAC: 2 apps 0 gls Total: 16 apps 6 gls

GRIEVE, James

Defender   5' 10"   13st 2lbs
Born: North Seaton, 13 January 1905
Died: Darlington, May 1984
Career: Seaton Delaval. Stakeford United. ASHINGTON March 1925. Seaton Delaval July 1925. Sheppey United 1925-26. ASHINGTON July 1926. Cramlington Village October 1928. Durham Divisional Police January 1929. East Cramlington Black Watch February 1930. Dudley United (Northam) August 1934.
Debut v Bradford Park Avenue (a) 9.10.26, lost 0-2
Said to have given "An admirable display at pivot" on his League debut, Grieve was even more successful during the second half of his first full campaign when introduced at right full-back in place of Ted Ferguson, who was seriously injured in the FA Cup-tie against Nottingham Forest on 8th January 1927. After completing 25 League matches in his first season, Grieve's first team opportunities became less frequent. Probably too versatile for his own good, he was able to occupy positions as diverse as full-back, centre-forward and all three half-back positions, without being able to hold down his first team place in any one role.
Appearances: FL: 43 apps 1gl Total: 43 apps 1 gl
Note: Although his birth certificate gives a surname Grieve, he was commonly known as Grieves, and this spelling appears throughout in the archives of the Football League.

GRIFFITHS, Thomas

Centre-forward
5' 9½"   11st 7lbs
Born: Willington Quay, July quarter 1901
Career: Willington St. Aidan's. Lincoln City August 1922. Jarrow February 1923. Trials with Darlington and Hartlepools United in 1923. ASHINGTON June 1923. Jarrow February 1924
Debut v Wrexham (a) 25.8.23, lost 0-4
Ashington's personnel for the 1923-24 campaign was almost entirely changed from that of the previous season, with only Robertson, Davidson, Price and Tubb of the 1922-23 campaign appearing on the books. Said to show clever touches in the pre season practice matches, Tommy Griffiths was one of nine new players to represent the Colliers in the season's opener at Wrexham. After a disappointing display all round in the 4-0 defeat at the Racecourse, the axe was wielded and a much changed eleven commenced, two days later, with a 3-1 home victory against new-comers to the League, Doncaster Rovers. Griffiths, who was replaced by Tom Robertson, did not get another first team opportunity. Earlier in his career, in less than a full season with Lincoln City, Griffiths was joint leading scorer with Harry Pringle, netting seven goals in 22 appearances.
Appearances: FL: 1 app 0 gls Total: 1 app 0 gls

GUTHRIE, George Robert

Goalkeeper
Born: Gateshead, 1 December 1899
Died: Pelton Fell, County Durham, 14 December 1981
Career: Scotswood. Sunderland "A" Team. Felling Colliery. West Stanley June 1923. ASHINGTON amateur October 1924. Chilton Colliery 1926. South Shields March 1926.
Debut v Crewe Alexandra (a) 18.10.24, lost 0-1

In two consecutive League outings as deputy for Tom Newton in October 1924, amateur George Guthrie proved a capable stand in. In both matches he was well shielded by rearguard pair Thompson and Hamilton, keeping the debit score down to three goals in two matches. At this point in the season, the Colliers main problems were in attack, as they scored only one goal in four matches during the month.

Appearances: FL: 2 apps 0 gls Total: 2 apps 0 gls

HALL, Thomas Henry

Inside-left   5' 7"   10st 2lbs
Born: Birtley, April quarter 1904
Career: Stobswood St. John's. ASHINGTON May 1922
Debut v Wigan Borough (a) 2.9.22, lost 1-6
Dubbed "The Chevington teenager" by the local correspondent, Tom Hall made a favourable impression in the pre-season practice match at Portland Park, scoring one goal in the "Reds" 5-3 win against the "Stripes". On his League debut, however, he had little chance to shine, as the Colliers were on the back foot from the outset of their opening fixture against Wigan Borough at Springfield Park. Hall was one of four players dropped for the return fixture and one week later a much improved team display earned a 2-1 win. Hall's second and final outing was in a 2-0 defeat at Nelson, who went on to lift the championship of the Northern Section.

Appearances: FL: 2 apps 0 gls Total: 2 apps 0 gls

HAMILTON, George William

Left-back
5' 9"   11st 10lbs
Born: Shankhouse *circa* 1899
Career: Newcastle-on-Tyne Schoolboys. Stakeford Albion. Watford (trial). Stakeford United. Blyth Spartans March 1920. ASHINGTON October 1921 to June 1928. (Shankhouse loan during 1923-24). Frickley Colliery

September 1928. South Kirkby Colliery August 1930. Shankhouse September 1934.
Debut v Accrington Stanley (a) 27.12.21, lost 0-3
Despite starring in schools football, George Hamilton had to wait patiently before establishing himself in League football. Possessing marked ability from an early age, he was not easily beaten and with youth on his side was always expected to develop into a sturdy and resourceful back. His first three seasons were spent mainly at reserve team level, but he then missed only five League matches in three seasons spanning 1924-27.

Appearances: FL: 162 Apps 0 gls FAC: 6 apps 0 gls Total: 168 apps 0 gls
Honours: England Schoolboy International v Scotland and Wales in 1913.

HARRIS, William James

Inside-right   5' 10"   12st 0lbs
Born: Cramlington, Northumberland, 25 April 1900
Died: Cramlington, 5 April 1969
Career: Whitley Bay Athletic. Coventry City August 1923. South Shields July 1924. Colwyn Bay United January 1925. Walker Celtic. ASHINGTON May 1926. Huddersfield Town March 1927. Wrexham October 1927. ASHINGTON August 1928 to June 1929.
Debut v Wigan Borough (a) 11.9.26, won 4-1 (scored two)
Bill Harris' first love was athletics and he developed into a sprinter good enough to win the £100 prize in the Northumberland Sprint Competition at Morpeth. His early football career was not distinguished as he had played only twice at League level prior to arriving at Portland Park. Two goals on his debut at Wigan Borough earned maximum points, but it proved to be an isolated success for the team who were particularly poor travellers throughout the season. A spell out of the side ended on November 13th, and his reintroduction sparked a run of improved form, and his individual contribution earned him a move to First Division Huddersfield Town in the following March. The Leeds Road side finished runners-up for the League championship in the same season, but Bill Harris failed to break into the first team and was allowed to join Wrexham after a brief seven-month stay. After two goals in 14

League and Cup games he returned to Portland Park for a second spell. Sadly, he was unable to replicate his earlier contribution (11 goals in 21 League matches), scoring just twice in 19 matches as the Colliers crashed out of the Football League.
Appearances: FL: 40 apps 13 gls FAC: 3 apps 0 gls Total: 43 apps 13 gls

HENDERSON, James

Inside-left
5' 7½" 10st 7lbs
Born: Newcastle-on-Tyne
Career: Scotswood. Cardiff City August 1913. Newcastle United May 1919, fee £50. Scotswood 1920. ASHINGTON July 1920. Scotswood August 1922. Spennymoor United January 1923.
Debut v Barrow (h) 15.10.21, lost 0-2
James Henderson commenced in senior football with Cardiff City, at that time members of the Southern League Division One. His best run of first team action spanned October and November 1913, when he scored in victories against Watford and Gillingham at Ninian Park. After the Great War and service with the Lancashire Fusiliers, a homeward move took him to Newcastle United. He scored the Magpies' first post-war goal in the Football League when he netted on his debut in the 1-0 win against Arsenal at Highbury on 30th August 1919, but he then failed to hold a first team place, dropping into non-league circles, initially with Scotswood, and then with Ashington for season 1920-21. Retained for the following season at Portland Park, Henderson nevertheless featured only once in League action, his debut coinciding with the Colliers' first home defeat as a Football League club.
Appearances: FL: 1 app 0 gls Total: 1 app 0 gls

HENDERSON, Thomas

Full-back/Wing-half 5' 11" 12st 4lbs
Born: Black Callerton, Northumberland.
Career: North Walbottle. Newcastle United January 1920. Leadgate Park June 1920. Workington June 1921. ASHINGTON June 1923. Annfield Plain July 1925 to August 1930. Wallsend March 1931.
Debut v Wrexham (a) 25.8.23, lost 0-4
Two seasons with the Colliers followed a strangely familiar pattern with lengthy spells of first team action being abruptly terminated following a 7-1 defeat by Wolverhampton Wanderers on 5th January 1923, and an identical 7-1 defeat by Bradford Park Avenue on 17th December 1924. In the earlier part of each season, the well-built defender gave sound displays, exclusively at right-back in his first season, and on both flanks in the middle line in 1924-25, when he chipped in with three League goals from open play. Henderson served in the Great War and was wounded in France. A brother, Henry, had trials with Bolton Wanderers when a White-le-Head player.
Appearances: FL: 40 apps 3 gls FAC: 5 apps 0 gls Total: 45 apps 3 gls
Note: There has been previous confusion regarding the careers of two players named Thomas Henderson, playing at about the same time. The player who played once for Hartlepools United in April 1926 was born at Lemington-on-Tyne and played for the local Glass Works team.

HEPPLE, Robert

Inside-left
5' 8" 10st 12lbs
Born: Mickley, 18 January 1898
Died: Mickley, April quarter 1970
Career: Mickley. Bradford City May 1920. Reading May 1921. Mickley cs 1922. ASHINGTON June 1923. West Wylam Colliery.
South Tyne Rangers (Haltwhistle) December 1927. ASHINGTON amateur March 1928.

Mickley September 1930. Prudhoe Castle Welfare October 1932.

Debut v Doncaster Rovers (a) 3.9.23, lost 1-2
Robert Hepple began as an outside-right and made his debut in the First Division with Bradford City in February 1921. He played in just three first team matches before joining Reading in May 1921, his spell at Valley Parade spent as understudy to Dickie Bond, the England International wingman. Hepple appeared in the first 17 matches of the season for Reading before losing his place, and was released into non-league football in the close season. He was one of thirteen professionals signed by Ashington in the summer of 1923, following the previous season's readmission application, and the bold recruitment policy paid some dividends, as the side finished the season in eighth position, their best ever placing in the Third Division North. Despite an extended run of ten consecutive matches in early season, it was Ernest Kidd, the former Wigan Borough outside-right, who dominated the first team right wing berth and Hepple moved on in the close season. He was recalled from non-league football, on amateur forms, in the late stages of season 1927-28 but added only two more first team appearances to his record. The first of which, a 3-0 defeat at Chesterfield, was played in a blinding snowstorm, play being suspended for eight minutes in the second half due to the severity of the storm. A fortnight later, his final League outing was a high scoring encounter at Tranmere Rovers, the home side winning 5-3.
Appearances: FL: 12 apps 1 gl Total: 12 apps 1 gl

HINE, John Robert A

Right-half
Born: Tynemouth, July quarter 1895
Career: ASHINGTON (A pre-League player) and registered for FL matches at the start of season 1921-22.
Debut v Durham City (a) 24.9.21, lost 0-1
Little is known about John Hine who appears in the Football League's registrations as a retained player from the previous season when the Colliers operated in the North-Eastern League and were winners of the Northumberland Senior Cup. Without an appearance in any of the pre-season practice matches, Hine was drafted in to the seniors for the first northern "Derby" at Durham City, when player-manager O'Connell was unfit to turn out, Knowles taking over at centre-half with Hine taking the right-half berth. In four previous meetings under North-Eastern League auspices, the Colliers held an unbeaten record against Durham, but in conditions more suited for cricket than football, the Dunelmians proved stronger in attack, although McCloud lost a fine opportunity of bringing the scores level near to the close.
Appearances: FL: 1 app 0 gls Total: 1 app 0 gls

HODGSON, Thomas

Centre-forward
Born: Northumberland
Career: Alnwick Town. ASHINGTON amateur November, professional December 1924
Debut v Wrexham (h) 20.12.24, won 2-0 (scored one)
The Colliers' eleven for the visit of Wrexham on 20th December 1924 was much changed from the side that had suffered a heavy 7-1 defeat at Bradford Park Avenue just three days earlier. Two players made their first appearance, Ridley in goal, and Hodgson at centre-forward. The reshuffled team were level at half-time and while Wrexham had long periods of ascendancy throughout, goals by Robertson and Hodgson, both following good work by Laverick, earned Ashington two welcome points. On Christmas Day, a side showing just one change travelled to Rotherham County and secured the season's first victory on the road. A hat-trick by Gardner and a second goal in two matches by Hodgson secured the points in a 4-1 victory. In the busy Christmas schedule, George Johnson was reintroduced at centre-forward for the trip to Chesterfield on 27th December, and he remained as attack leader for the remainder of the season, scoring 15 League goals in just 22 matches.
Appearances: FL: 2 apps 2 gls Total: 2 apps 2 gls

HOFFMAN, Ernest Henry (Also known as Holt)

Goalkeeper   5' 7"   11st 2lbs
Born: Wakefield, 16 July 1892
Died: South Shields, 20 January 1959
Career: Boldon School. Hebburn Wesleyans. Hebburn Old Boys. Hebburn Argyle 1914. South Shields amateur. Wartime guest player with Tottenham Hotspur. South Shields amateur January 1919, professional March 1920. Derby County April 1923. ASHINGTON August 1923. Darlington August 1924. Wood Skinners F.C. (Hebburn) October 1925. York City August 1929. Jarrow secretary-manager *circa* September 1926. Blyth Spartans secretary-manager May 1933 to 1937. Birmingham scout May 1937 to 1939. South Shields secretary April 1939 to October 1946.
Debut v Wrexham (a) 25.8.23, lost 0-4
Of German descent and a pork butcher by trade, Hoffman was born in Wakefield, moving to South Shields to live with an uncle. He was capped by England at amateur level before the First World War, played once for Tottenham Hotspur and then spent some time as an internee. Joining South Shields in 1919 he made 20 Second Division appearances before joining Derby County, where he played in just one League match, the final fixture of season1922-23. Despite a shaky opening with the Colliers – a 4-0 defeat at Wrexham – Hoffman generally held off the challenge of Davidson for the first team jersey. On Boxing Day 1923 he had the unusual experience of conceding a goal, from a penalty that was scored by a fellow custodian. This came in a 1-1 draw at New Brighton, whose Irish international goalkeeper Bert Mehaffy was relieved of his role in the following February after shooting wide from the spot against Doncaster Rovers and having to get back down the field in undignified haste.
Appearances: FL: 35 apps 0 gls FAC: 4 apps 0 gls Total: 39 apps 0 gls
Honours: England Amateur International, 2 caps 1914.

HOPPER, Matthew

Outside-right 5' 6"   10st 10lbs
Born: Ashington, 17 January 1893
Died: Ashington, January quarter 1978
Career: Annfield Plain. Esh Winning September 1914. Percy Main Colliery Welfare. ASHINGTON 1919-20. Lincoln City July 1920. Millwall April 1921, fee £550. Catford South End August 1924. Coventry City August 1926. ASHINGTON August 1927. Annfield Plain November 1928. Northfleet United 1929. Consett October 1930 to February 1931. West Moor Welfare November 1931.
Debut v Bradford City (h) 27.8.27, drawn 2-2
Popularly known as "Monty", Hopper served aboard a minesweeper in World War One. Following hostilities, his first spell with Ashington ended in July 1920, as Pat O'Connell, the Irish International, was just one of more than a dozen new players recruited. The ground was also terraced on three sides, as all was made ready for a season that ended with a successful application for entry into the Football League. Hopper migrated to Lincoln City, and brought a useful fee when transferred to Millwall after less than a season with the Midland League club. The diminutive wingman made his first appearance in League football on 30th April 1921 in a 1-0 home defeat by Southampton, and in a further two seasons he totalled 48 League appearances, scoring just one goal. A spell in non-League football preceded a season with Coventry City in which he made 17 League and Cup appearances and scored one goal. A second spell with the Colliers commenced in August 1927 and he made a good start. On his debut, the Colliers had the advantage of the wind and sun in the first half and they managed the light ball better than Bradford

City. Randall opened the scoring after two minutes, and on 13 minutes a centre from Hopper was cleverly headed home by Ball. A number of injuries disrupted the Colliers in the second half, Chipperfield was forced to retire and although Grieve continued after injury he was a limping figure and unable to contribute very much thereafter. To add to the catalogue of injuries, goalkeeper Ridley damaged a finger when in collision with a Bradford City forward. It was not surprising that the Colliers sacrificed a point having been so depleted. Hopper retained his first team place for all but one match until mid season. Ironically, he scored against Southport on December 24th, in what proved to be his final senior outing before being replaced by Charles Robinson.

Appearances: FL: 19 apps 1 gl FAC: 2 apps 0 gls Total: 21 apps 1 gl

HUNTER, Norman

Inside-right
5' 7½" 12st 0lbs
Born: Sheepwash,
July quarter 1905
Career: Wreckenden
Blue Star. Blyth
Spartans February
1923. ASHINGTON
amateur March 1923.
Washington Colliery December 1926. Sheffield United January 1929. Washington Colliery August 1930. ASHINGTON September 1931. Blyth Spartans May 1932. Chopwell Institute August 1933.
Debut v Walsall (h) 17.3.23, won 3-0 (scored one)
Following two heavy defeats (7-4 at Grimsby Town and 5-2 at home against Accrington Stanley) a number of team changes were made. A brief report in the *Newcastle Journal* confirmed that the Colliers had shown a welcome improvement in defeating Walsall by three clear goals. Norman Hunter, a late season arrival from Blyth Spartans, opened the scoring on his League debut and his introduction, along with another amateur, Albert Tubb, had much to do with the team's increased efficiency. Norman Hunter's brother Robert also assisted Ashington, but not in Football League

matches. Norman's brief spell with Sheffield United did not include any first team involvement.

Appearances: FL: 9 apps 1 gl Total: 9 apps 1 gl

HUTCHINSON, Robert

Inside-right
5' 8½" 11st 9lbs
Born: Gosforth, Newcastle-on-Tyne, 22 December 1894
Died: Gosforth, July quarter 1971
Career: Gosforth. Palmer's (Jarrow). St. Mirren August 1914. Wartime guest player with ASHINGTON January 1915. Newcastle United amateur January, professional May 1919. ASHINGTON May 1920. Nelson May 1922. Stockport County January 1924, in exchange for Doug Humphrey. Chesterfield May 1924. Barrow July 1925. In season 1926-27 played in the USA and assisted New Bedford Whalers, Springfield Babes, Fall River Marksmen and Newark Skeeters. In 1927-28 played in eleven matches with Hartford Americans. Darlington March 1928. West Stanley September 1928. Gosforth & Coxlodge British Legion amateur September 1930.
Debut v Grimsby Town (a) 3.9.21, lost 1-6
Bobby Hutchinson made his Football League debut with Ashington, having failed to reach senior level with Newcastle United. In earliest days an inside-forward, he scored his first goal for the Colliers after 30 seconds versus Durham City at Portland Park on 1st October 1921. Joining Nelson in May 1922 and immediately installed at outside-left, he made maximum appearances in his first season when the Seedhill club won the championship of the Northern Section. At his best, the Geordie wingman was a dangerous opponent having excellent ball control, a good turn of speed, and the ability to centre accurately on the run. If he had a fault, it surrounded his occasional tendency to try to beat three or four men, with the inevitable

result. After completing 137 League appearances and 11 goals for five different clubs he then spent two years in American football. Returning to add just three more League appearances with Darlington, he was still operating in non-League football in his 36th year.

Appearances: FL: 22 apps 4 gls Total: 22 apps 4 gls

Honours: Nelson: Division Three North champions 1923.

IONS, William Todd

Inside-left
Born: Bellingham, Northumberland, January quarter 1906
Died: Germany, 7 April 1942
Career: Bedlington United. White-le-Head Rangers. West Stanley July 1925. Newcastle United Swifts. Annfield Plain June 1926. Preston Colliery August 1927. ASHINGTON amateur 22nd August, professional 29th August 1928. St Peter's Albion January 1930. Crook Town August 1930. Also with Chester-le-Street at some point but dates untraced.
Debut v Southport (a) 25.8.28, lost 1-2

One of a pair of inside-forwards signed by Ashington in late August 1928, the other, William James "Bill" Harris, returned to Portland Park after service with Huddersfield Town and Wrexham. Thomas Ions had filled a variety of positions with Preston Colliery in 1927-28, but he was signed to operate at inside-left to Randall, filling the gap left by the departure of Billy Watson, after five years and exactly two hundred League appearances. Ions held the inside-left spot for much of the first half of the season, but a run of ten matches without a win brought a number of changes, John Carlton being the preferred choice at inside-left for much of the second half of the season. Ions served with the Northumberland Fusiliers in World War Two, and an unconfirmed report suggested that he had died there whilst held as a prison of war.

Appearances: FL: 21 apps 2 gls FAC: 1 app 0 gls Total: 22 apps 2 gls

JOHNSON, George Alfred

Centre-forward/Wing half-back
5' 9"   11st 0lbs
Born: Ashington, 20 July 1904
Died: Reading, 26 May 1985
Career: Ashington Welfare. Bedlington United. ASHINGTON October 1924. Sheffield Wednesday July 1929, fee £500. Reading June 1932, fee £90. Watford May 1937. Krooger F.C. (Holland) coach October 1946. Gauda (Holland) coach to November 1949. Chelsea scout (very briefly). Oxford United coach November 1949, later grounds man until retirement.
Debut v Crewe Alexandra (a) 18.10.24, lost 0-1

George Johnson scored in each of his first three matches when handed the role of attack leader in late December 1924 and at the close of his first season in the Colliers' colours he had scored 15 goals in 22 League matches. Had he retained the position throughout his five seasons of League football his goal tally would doubtless have far exceeded 68, but he spent lengthy spells in the half-back line in three of his five seasons at Portland Park. When playing in the attack he was a clever and dangerous tactician with a fine shot. When filling a half-back role he was conspicuous for his constructive work and prompting. Typically, in season 1927-28, he was first selected at centre-forward on December 3rd at Nelson and scored twice in a 5-1 win. By the end of the season he had scored 24 goals his total including five "doubles" and hat-tricks against Wigan Borough and Nelson. He was the last Ashington player to score a hat-trick in the Football League in a 3-1 win at Hartlepools United on 9th March 1929 and his total might have been four, but he missed from a penalty kick when the score was 2-0. Leaving the Colliers as they crashed out of the Football League, he found himself in elevated company when he joined Sheffield Wednesday, current League and Central League Champions. In three seasons at

Hillsborough he began by scoring 29 goals for the reserves in 1929-30 and 59 Central League goals overall, but played in only one First Division match, a 4-0 win at Blackpool, in which he scored one goal. Moving on to Reading in June 1932 he netted a hat-trick against Northampton Town on his debut, but was almost immediately switched to right-half, a position that he retained throughout 161 League appearances. He was Reading's captain when they reached the 5th Round of the FA Cup in 1935 and lost narrowly to the season's League Champions Arsenal, Cliff Bastin scoring the only goal of the game. Johnson's final League club was Watford, and although he was signed with a view to captaining their reserve side, he played in 23 League matches and scored eight goals. The outbreak of World War Two effectively terminated his playing career but he remained in the game in a coaching capacity in Holland in early post war years. His hobbies were listed as tennis and gardening and in retirement he settled in Reading.

Appearances: FL: 167 apps 67 gls FAC: 7 apps 1 gl Total: 174 apps 68 gls

KIDD, Ernest

Outside-right
5' 9½" 11st 6lbs
Born: Tynemouth, 25 May 1895
Died: Dunston-on-Tyne, July quarter 1974
Career: Scotswood. Newcastle United amateur October 1919. Dunston Atlas Villa. Bolton Wanderers August 1920. Wigan Borough March 1922. ASHINGTON June 1923. Workington May 1924.
Debut v Wrexham (a) 25.8.23, lost 0-4
A solidly built winger who, despite early association with Newcastle United and Bolton Wanderers, did not feature in League football until joining Wigan Borough in the late months of their first season as a Football League club. He was retained for 1922-23 and at the close of that season, with his record standing at 26 appearances and one goal, he was released and joined the Colliers.

He took some time to re-establish himself after being replaced by Robert Hepple after the opening three matches of the season. Returning to first team duty on December 22nd against New Brighton he was outstanding in a 5-0 victory and retained his place in the side for much of the remainder of the season. The 1923-24 campaign proved to be the Colliers best, as they finished eighth in the League and their extended run in the FA Cup was an additional bonus. Four ties attracted well over 22,000 spectators in total with 11,837 present at Portland Park for the visit of First Division giants, Aston Villa. The receipts for this match amounting to a very welcome £806-10s-0d.

Appearances: FL: 28 apps 0 gls FAC: 2 apps 0 gls Total: 30 apps 0 gls

KIRKUP, Richard

Right-half   5' 7½"   11st 3lbs
Born: Ashington, 7 April 1908
Died: Bedford, April 1988
Career: Ashington Welfare. ASHINGTON trial August 1926, amateur January 1927, registered for FL matches, again as an amateur, October 1927. Carlisle United (illegally) September-October 1928. Bedlington United November 1928. Annfield Plain June 1929. Newbiggin West End September 1933.
Debut v Darlington (a) 15.10.27, lost 1-5
A local amateur who spent much of season 1927-28 in the reserve side, deputising at right-half in three matches in October 1927, and in two games at inside-right in December. Two other locally born players, Joe Coombs and John Carlton were the ones who dominated in Kirkup's preferred position at right-half.

Appearances: FL: 5 apps 0 gls Total: 5 apps 0 gls

KNOWLES, Frank

Half-back
5' 11"   12st 7lbs
Born: Hyde, Cheshire, April quarter 1891
Died: Hyde, Cheshire, 20 January 1951
Career: Hyde St Thomas. Hyde F.C. Stalybridge Celtic cs 1911. Manchester United December 1911. Skelmersdale United. Sandbach Ramblers December 1925. Wartime guest player with Hyde, Arsenal and Oldham Athletic. Hartlepools United August 1919. Manchester City October 1919. Stalybridge Celtic during November 1919. ASHINGTON August 1921. Stockport County May 1922. Newport County June 1923. Queens Park Rangers February 1924. Ashton National June 1926. Macclesfield September 1926. Hyde United Committee June 1933.
Debut v Grimsby Town (a) 3.9.21, lost 1-6
Frank Knowles left his employment in the cotton mills of Lancashire to become a professional footballer with Manchester United. Initially he had to be content with a place in the reserve team, but it was a very strong side, remaining undefeated in 26 matches in 1911-12 when the Central League championship was won. In the same season, Knowles had his first chance in the League side, an injury to England International centre-half Charlie Roberts enabling him to feature in seven late-season matches. In November of the following season he was fortunate to escape serious injury, when he was one of six passengers in a car that crashed and overturned near to Rudyard Lake in Staffordshire. Two of the passengers were killed instantly but Knowles escaped with nothing more than a severe shaking. The outbreak of World War One interrupted his career, just at a time when he was enjoying some lengthy spells of first team football. He enlisted in the RGA and whilst training at Aldershot played for Arsenal in the London Combination. On his return to civilian life he played briefly for Hartlepools United and then joined Manchester City, but his association was a brief one and he then embarked on a wandering path that took in clubs in both the Northern and Southern Sections of Division Three. His Ashington season commenced with a crushing defeat at Grimsby Town, but he retained his place in the side throughout most of the season. His robust style and strength in the air, coupled with good constructive ideas, made him an outstanding figure in the Colliers defence in their first season in the Football League. His playing days ended in the Cheshire County League and he then became 'mine host' at the Sportsman's Hotel, Hyde.
Appearances: FL: 34 apps 3 gls FAC: 4 apps 0 gls Total: 38 apps 3 gls

LATIMER, John George

Goalkeeper
Born: Newcastle-on-Tyne, 10 November 1904
Died: Newcastle-on-Tyne, 7 June 1977
Career: Tod's Nook School. Prudhoe Street Mission. Benwell Colliery. ASHINGTON amateur October 1928, professional January 1929. Benwell Colliery August 1929. Washington Colliery November 1929. Benwell Colliery November 1930.
Debut v South Shields (h) 25.12.28, lost 1-3
In a brief but busy association with the Colliers, Latimer took over from Bill Bradley in mid season 1928-29. He joined a side in terminal decline, and with no prior senior experience he was inclined to be erratic at times, but strove manfully to guard his goal as the team headed for the relegation trapdoor. He conceded an average of close to three goals per game in his 22 outings, particularly heavy defeats being sustained at home to Doncaster Rovers (4-7) and at Crewe Alexandra (0-7). The team also conceded five goals without reply at Rochdale and at home to Crewe Alexandra.
Appearances: FL: 22 apps 0 gls Total: 22 apps 0 gls

LAVERICK, William

Outside-left
5' 6½" 11st 2lbs
Born: Pelton Fell, 11 September 1897
Died: Murton Seaham, 24 June 1975
Career: Pelton Fell. Annfield Plain June 1919. Darlington cs 1920. Chester-le-Street July 1921. ASHINGTON July 1923. Annfield Plain September 1925. West Stanley. ASHINGTON August 1926. Halifax Town September 1928. Murton Colliery Welfare May 1929 (and still with them in 1933).
Debut v Wrexham (a) 25.8.23, lost 0-4

On the small side, but solidly built, Bill Laverick was a speedy and accomplished outside-left who gave Third Division defenders lots of trouble in his first two seasons at Portland Park. Generally with Billy Watson as his inside partner, Laverick missed only one match throughout his first season, scoring nine goals. He was similarly consistent in his second campaign, playing in 40 matches and scoring five goals. After a season spent with Annfield Plain, the Colliers came to an agreement with their old left winger to spend a third season at Portland Park. During his absence, however, his former inside partner Billy Watson had been switched to outside-left and he continued to hold the position despite Laverick's return, restricting him to just ten matches in 1926-27. A move to Halifax Town brought up his century of senior appearances but only just, as he only played twice during his season at the Shay.

Appearances: FL: 92 apps 13 gls FAC: 6 apps 2 gls Total: 98 apps 15 gls

LOUGHRAN, Thomas Henry

Centre-half 5' 8½" 11st 4lbs
Born: Sunderland, January quarter 1904
Died: Sunderland, 5 October 1957
Career: Usworth Colliery. ASHINGTON January 1923. Workington May 1923. Usworth Colliery March 1924. Sunderland West End. Carlisle United May 1925. Spennymoor United August 1926. Usworth Colliery. St Joseph's C.Y.M.S. (Sunderland) December 1934.
Debut v Wrexham (h) 20.1.23, drawn 1-1

One of seven different centre-halves fielded by the Colliers during 1922-23. Tom Loughran took over from Joe Morton in mid season, but the Usworth Colliery recruit failed to impress in seven consecutive outings that yielded just four points with an adverse goal average of 12-21. Happily, the problem position was solved in March by the signing of the stylish and effective Scot, Jimmy Price from Nelson, who went on to amass a club record 244 first team outings.

Appearances: FL: 7 apps 0 gls Total: 7 apps 0 gls

McCLOUD, Thomas Edward

Outside-left   5' 8½"   10st 12lbs
Born: Broomhill, 21 January 1898
Died: Northumberland South, September 1986
Career: Chevington. Amble. ASHINGTON amateur June, professional September 1921 to cs 1923.
Debut v Wrexham (a) 10.9.21. lost 0-2
Tom McCloud possessed pace and dribbling ability and he enjoyed an excellent first season on the Colliers' left flank. He was similarly effective as 1922-23 opened, being on the mark in the season's first home match, a 2-1 win against Wigan Borough. Sadly, his luck ran out on 30th December 1922 when he was injured at Rochdale and remained sidelined until 3rd February. Despite scoring on his return at Crewe Alexandra he failed to re-establish himself, Foster being switched over to outside-left, with Soulsby taking over on the opposite flank. McCloud did not appear at senior level after February 10th, and he was not retained at the end of the season.
Appearances: FL: 45 apps 4 gls FAC: 5 apps 0 gls Total: 50 apps 4 gls

McGILL, Thomas

Inside-left   5' 10"   11st 7lbs
Born: Wallsend, 28 July 1901
Died: Horncastle, 19 July 1979
Career: St. Luke's. Scotswood November 1919. ASHINGTON May 1921. Wallsend Town cs 1922. Cardiff City March 1923. Scotswood. Shildon July 1924. Kettering Town July 1924. West Stanley August 1925. Ebbw Vale 1925. Charlton Athletic May 1927. North Walbottle January 1928. Lovells Athletic cs 1928.
Debut v Grimsby Town (h) 27.8.21. won 1-0
Opposed to a hefty and uncompromising Grimsby Town side, Ashington nevertheless marked their Football League debut with a hard-fought victory. Both McGill and Dickinson were knocked out during the course of a bruising encounter. Dickinson, scorer of the winning goal, was forced to retire but the ten men held out to ensure an excellent beginning to life in League circles. McGill failed to impress in six early season matches, although he scored twice in his final first team outing, a 6-0 win against Close

Works in the FA Cup, fourth qualifying round. Sadly, his season was brought to a premature end when, in a reserve team match at Bedlington United on 21st January 1922, he was carried from the field with a broken leg. In terms of League football, McGill spent a season in reserve with Cardiff City and later appeared in five Third Division matches with Charlton Athletic.
Appearances: FL: 6 apps 0 gls FAC: 1 app 2 gls Total: 7 apps 2 gls
Honours: Ebbw Vale: Welsh Cup winners 1926.

MAHON, Patrick

Right-back   5' 8"   11st 7lbs
Born: Walker, Newcastle-on-Tyne, 27 February 1896
Died: Walker, Newcastle-on-Tyne, October quarter 1975
Career: Wallsend. ASHINGTON July 1922. Gosforth & Coxbridge British Legion August 1926.
Debut v Wigan Borough (a) 26.8.22, lost 1-6
Recruited from Wallsend along with Joe Morton, the pair made their Football League debuts together in the heavy opening day defeat at Wigan Borough. While Morton was quickly replaced at centre-half, Mahon enjoyed lengthy spells of first team football, mainly in a full-back pairing with Harry Featherstone. Mahon kicked accurately and tackled well, and after eleven matches had three goals to his credit. All were as a result of penalty kicks, but he lost the job after shooting over the bar against Barrow on 23rd December. Unfortunately, his replacements did no better, Featherstone and Foster both missing from the spot later in the season. Mahon spent only one season with the Colliers and an unconfirmed report suggested that he was next with Shildon.
Appearances: FL: 24 apps 3 gls FAC: 1 app 0 gls Total: 25 apps 3 gls

MALLOY, William

Outside-right
5' 8½" 11st 7lbs
Born: Benwell,
April quarter 1903
Died: Newcastle-on-Tyne, July
quarter 1967
Career: Benwell
Colliery. Spen Black
& White.
Northampton Town
(trial) August, professional September 1924.
Spen Black & White 1925. ASHINGTON May
1926. Stockport County July 1927. Annfield
Plain (trial) November 1928.
Debut v New Brighton (a) 28.8.26, lost 0-4
A speedy outside-right with a good shot,
Malloy was quickly off the mark, netting his
first goal in his second appearance for the
Colliers, a 1-1 draw against Wrexham, in the
first home match of season 1926-27. He was
also on the mark on Christmas Day, scoring
both goals in the surprise 2-0 win at Durham
City. A move to Stockport County provided
him with fewer opportunities at senior level.
The strong County side, spearheaded by the
former Bolton Wanderers centre-forward Joe
Smith, (who scored 40 goals in 42 matches),
finished third in the Northern Section.
Malloy's nine League appearances proved to
be his last in senior football.
Appearances: FL: 31 apps 6 gls FAC: 3 apps 0
gls Total: 34 apps 6 gls

MOORE, David

Goalkeeper   5' 9½"   11st 2lbs
Born: Ashington
Career: Ashington Welfare. ASHINGTON
amateur August 1926, professional August
1927. Wallaw United October 1928. Walsall
(trial) September 1930. Ashington Colliery
Electricians February 1932. Ellington United
January 1936. Ashington Colliery
Electricians October 1936.
Debut v Crewe Alexandra (h) 29.8.27, lost 0-2
Local amateur goalkeeper David Moore was
kept busy on his League debut, visitors
Crewe Alexandra showing much better
combination leading the local correspondent
to consider: "In every department, Crewe
were superior to the home side". Continually
brought into action behind a defence that
was given too much to do, Moore earned
praise for keeping the score down to a
respectable level. All this was to change,
however, when the unfortunate custodian
conceded six goals at New Brighton and six
again at Halifax Town, and all within the
space of one week, truly a goalkeeper's
nightmare!
Appearances: FL: 3 apps 0 gls Total: 3 apps 0
gls

MORTON, Joseph

Centre-half
5' 10½" 12st 2lbs
Born: Newcastle-on-Tyne
Career: St Peter's Albion. Wallsend.
ASHINGTON June 1922. Wallsend August
1923. A. Reyrolla & Co FC Committee June
1934.
Debut v Wigan Borough (a) 26.8.22, lost 1-6
Although Joe Morton was said to have done
some useful work on his League debut,
Wigan Borough's centre-forward Dennison,

who scored four goals, proved a tough proposition. Filling the centre-half vacated by Irish International player-manager Pat O'Connell proved a very tall order, no fewer than seven different players occupied the vital role during the season, which ended in a re-election application. Ashington shipped 77 goals during the season, the worst defensive record of any club in the Division. Returning to Wallsend for a second spell after his season with the Colliers, Morton was still assisting them some thirteen years later.
Appearances: FL: 9 apps 0 gls Total: 9 apps 0 gls

MORTON, Robert

Outside-left   5' 9"   11st 0lbs
Born: Widdrington, Northumberland, 3 March 1906
Died: Widdrington, Northumberland, April 1990
Career: Widdrington.   Newbiggin. ASHINGTON amateur December 1922, professional July 1925. Bedlington United September 1926. Barnsley October 1927. Nottingham Forest May 1928. Newark Town June 1930. Bradford Park Avenue May 1931. Port Vale May 1932. Throckley Welfare July 1935. Blyth Spartans May 1936. Jarrow November 1936. Blyth Spartans. North Shields May 1939.
Debut v Barrow (h) 23.12.22, lost 2-6
The 6-2 defeat sustained by the Colliers on the occasion of Bob Morton's debut was not the heaviest defeat of the season – that occurred on the opening Saturday at Wigan Borough – but it was at that time their heaviest defeat at Portland Park under League auspices. One point from the previous five matches led to sweeping team changes. Since the previous match against Lincoln City, seven new players were introduced involving eight positions. Not surprisingly, there was a lack of understanding and little semblance of combined effort in the home side who, for three-quarters of the match, were five goals in arrears. With the Ashington half-backs unable to contain a faster forward opposition, they were unable to offer any meaningful support to their forward colleagues, Morton had a quiet debut but was unlucky on one occasion when his shot

struck the upright with Barrow's goalkeeper Carter well beaten. An apprentice colliery surveyor during his Ashington days, Morton did little with either Ashington or Barnsley, but scored four goals in 36 appearances for Nottingham Forest and 19 goals in 101 League appearances for Port Vale.
Appearances: 3 apps 0 gls Total: 3 apps 0 gls

NEWTON, Tom

Goalkeeper   5' 11"   11st 4lbs
Born: Ryton-on-Tyne
Career: Blaydon United. Croydon Common cs 1912. Swindon Town 1915. Scotswood. Portsmouth October 1919. Scotswood September 1923. ASHINGTON June 1924. Crawcrook Albion February 1926. Darlington September 1928 to 1929. Runswick FC November 1933.
Debut v Chesterfield (h) 30.8.24, won 2-1
Tom Newton served in the Footballer's Battalion in World War One and was taken as a prisoner of war. He resumed his football career with Portsmouth, initially as reserve to Ned Robson as Pompey won the championship of the Southern League, on goal average over Watford. Ironically, it was not until his last season at Fratton Park that Newton claimed the first team jersey, making 40 Appearances in 1922-23 as Portsmouth finished seventh in Division Three South. A season with Scotswood followed before he commenced as the last line of the Colliers' defence in August 1924. Initially said to "Guard the breach with fine judgment and intuition" he was nevertheless on the receiving end of a number of heavy defeats, particularly away from home, and a 7-1 defeat at Bradford Park Avenue on 17th December 1924 resulted in his replacement by reserve goalkeeper, Ralph Ridley. Inspired displays by his deputy ensured that he retained the first team jersey for the remainder of the season.
Appearances: FL: 16 apps 0 gls FAC: 2 apps 0 gls Total: 18 apps 0 gls

NICHOLSON, James

Centre-half
Born: Morpeth, 15 March 1901
Died: Morpeth, January quarter 1979
Career: East Northumberland Schoolboys. Heart of Midlothian (trial) February 1920. ASHINGTON amateur August, professional September 1922.
Debut v Lincoln City (h) 9.12.22, lost 0-2
The Colliers' management faced the second season of League football with some anxiety. A four-figure loss in the previous term compelled the Directors to be wary of a heavy wage bill. Departures included Knowles to Stockport County, Hutchinson to Nelson, Barber to Workington, Thompson to Luton Town, while player-manager O'Connell departed in the summer to commence on a coaching career. Halves Knowles and O'Connell were two very experienced campaigners, and during the season they were never successfully replaced, former England Schools International Nicholson being just one of seven different players who occupied the vital role of centre-half throughout a disappointing season that ended with the side having to apply for re-election. They had prospered in the first two months of the campaign, but the advent of heavier pitches exposed a lack of weight and stamina in the defence that was breached on 77 occasions in League matches, the worst defensive record in the Division.
Appearances: FL: 3 apps 0 gls Total: 3 apps 0 gls
Honours: Captained England Schoolboys in matches against Scotland and Wales in 1914.

NOBLE, James Frame

Inside-right
Born: Morpeth, 21 March 1905
Died: Morpeth, April quarter 1988
Career: ASHINGTON amateur October 1927.
Debut v Wrexham (a) 5.11.27, lost 1-5
Billed as "The Morpeth sprinter" on his debut and single League outing, Noble was unable to turn the tide of heavy away defeats that kept the Colliers anchored in the lower reaches of the table throughout the season. Thankfully, a late burst of form lifted the side to safety and 18th place in the table. In what was obviously a severe winter, terrible conditions prevailed at Wrexham, half a gale blowing, while rain fell heavily. Struggling in the teeth of a fierce wind in the first half, the Colliers were three goals behind at the interval. In a more even second half, Randall netted a good goal for Ashington, but Wrexham centre-forward Cecil Smith completed his hat-trick to give the home side victory by 5-1. At this point in the season, Ashington had conceded no fewer than 31 goals in seven away matches, and they continued to be poor travellers throughout, winning only once, at Nelson, by 5-1 on December 3rd, 1927.
Appearances: FL: 1 app 0 gls Total: 1 app 0 gls

O'CONNELL, Patrick Joseph

Centre-half   5' 11"   12st 0lbs
Born: Dublin, 8 March 1887
Died: St Pancras, London, 27 February 1959, age 71
Career: Frankfort F.C. (Dublin). Strandville Juniors 1908. Belfast Celtic amateur September 1908. Sheffield Wednesday March 1909, for a joint fee of £50, along with Peter Warren. Hull City May 1912, fee £350. Manchester United, loan April, professional May 1914, fee £1,000. Wartime guest player

with Clapton Orient, Rochdale & Chesterfield Municipal. Dumbarton August 1919, fee £200. ASHINGTON May 1920, appointed player-manager May 1921 to June 1922.Real Racing Club De Santander, coach cs 1922. Real Oviedo, coach 1929. Betis Balompie (Seville), coach 1932. FC Barcelona, coach cs 1935. Betis Balompie (Seville), coach 1940. CF Seville, coach 1942. Betis Balompie (Seville), coach 1945 to 1947, when he returned to CF Seville as a scout.

Debut v Grimsby Town (h) 27.8.21, won 1-0

Certainly the most celebrated of Ashington's 120 Football League players with five international caps that included appearances in all three of the 1913-14 home international matches when Ireland won the championship for the first time. One of a family of nine children and a glass fitter by trade, O'Connell began as a centre-forward with Belfast Celtic, but was successfully converted to half-back after joining Sheffield Wednesday following protracted wrangling over a transfer fee, eventually settled at £50 for O'Connell plus another player. Despite winning the first two of his international caps, against England and Scotland in February and March 1912, he had made only 21 League and Cup appearances for Wednesday who made a handsome profit when they transferred him to Hull City. Two years on, Manchester United paid £1,000 for his services, replacing one Irish International with another, Micky Hamill having returned to Belfast Celtic in the same close season. He arrived at Old Trafford fresh from international success and scored United's only goal on his debut, a 3-1 defeat by Oldham Athletic. After 35 League and Cup appearances he made guest appearances for Rochdale, Clapton Orient and Chesterfield during the World War One years, moving to Scotland to assist Dumbarton in August 1919. He joined Ashington on 11th May 1920 and was selected for the North-Eastern League representative eleven in January 1921. During the season, the Northumberland Senior Cup was won, Newcastle United being beaten in the final. Appointed team player-manager prior to the Colliers debut season in the Football League, O'Connell was nearing the end of his playing days at 35 years of age, but he safely guided his team through their first season and to a satisfactory tenth place finish in the table. Despite a relatively successful season, a loss of four figures was sustained and a curtailment of expenditure resulted in the departure of several of the club's better players. These included Knowles, Hutchinson, Barber, Thompson and, most significantly, Pat O'Connell. Most of the new signings were from local leagues and many were found wanting and the club had the unenviable experience of having to apply for readmission to the League at the close of their second season. O'Connell had in the meantime embarked on what proved to be an outstanding coaching career. Highlights of which included his winning of the La Liga Championship in 1935 with Betis Balompie (subsequently re-named Real Betis), a feat that earned him a three-year term with Catalan giants Barcelona. He was widely credited with assisting his club to survive the turmoil of the Spanish Civil War and guided them to the championship of the Catalonian League in 1936, and the Mediterranean League in 1937.

Appearances: FL: 19 apps 1 gl FAC: 4 apps 0 gls Total: 23 apps 1 gl

Honours: Irish International, 5 caps 1912-14. (He captained Ireland to their first British championship in season 1913-14). Irish Victory International v Scotland in March 1919.

Represented the North Eastern League v the Central League at Newcastle on 22 January 1921.

PAGE, George

Left-back
5' 9"   11st 12lbs
Born: Darlington, July quarter 1898
Career: Rise Carr. Doncaster Rovers March 1921. Barnsley May 1921. Accrington Stanley May 1922. ASHINGTON July 1923. Lincoln City July 1924. CreweAlexandra June 1926. York City August 1927.

Debut v Wrexham (a) 25.8.23, lost 0-4

In amateur days George Page captained Rise Carr and was first signed as a professional by Doncaster Rovers, before they gained Football League entry. Well built and speedy, his first spell of regular League football came with Accrington Stanley (31 appearances and one goal). A popular and reliable defender during his season with the Colliers, the first of his two goals came against one of his former clubs, Doncaster Rovers. Page was a more than useful emergency goalkeeper and performed with great credit when replacing Hoffman, who had dislocated his collar-bone, in a 2-0 defeat at Lincoln City in March 1924. Four months later, Page joined Lincoln City, where he earned the soubriquet "Deadshot George" after he had scored from the penalty spot in three consecutive matches in 1925-26. His League career ended with Crewe Alexandra, his career aggregate figures were 149 League matches and seven goals.

Appearances: FL: 36 apps 2 gls FAC: 4 apps 0 gls Total: 40 apps 2 gls

PIGG, William

Wing-half   5' 7½"   11st 6lbs
Born: High Spen, 27 January 1898
Died: Ashington, January quarter 1976
Career: Hamsterley School. Hamsterley Institute 1912. Chopwell Institute 1914. Hamsterley Juniors 1918. Spen Black & White 1919. ASHINGTON amateur October, professional November 1921. Queens Park Rangers July 1924. Carlisle United July 1926. Accrington Stanley June 1930 to May 1931.
Debut v Crewe Alexandra (a) 22.10.21, won 2-1

Bill Pigg began in junior football as an outside-left and represented the Durham Valley Schools League in matches against the schoolboy teams of Sunderland, Newcastle, Darlington and Ryton. He joined the army in 1915 when 17 years of age and was twice wounded during active service. After demobilisation he joined Hamsterley Juniors. They were actually a senior team and in his season with them they won the championship of the Durham Valley Senior League. During two seasons with Spen Black & White he was a Tynemouth Infirmary Cup winner, a finalist in the Newcastle Infirmary Cup and he also represented the Alliance against Chopwell in 1921. He began with the Colliers as captain of the reserve team but was quickly selected for the first team, where he remained a fixture. In his final season, Bill missed only two matches when the Colliers finished eighth in the table, their best position in League football. Queens Park Rangers signed him after they had experienced their worst-ever League season in 1923-24, but he left after two unrewarding campaigns, at the close of which the Rangers had to seek re-election for the second time in three seasons. A four-year stint with Carlisle United followed, and he played in the Cumbrians' first Football League match, a 3-2 win at Accrington Stanley on 25th August 1928. Two years later he wound up his senior career with Stanley. Bill Pigg gave yeoman service to each of his senior clubs, totalling 193 League appearances and nine goals.

Appearances: FL: 95 apps 1 gl FAC: 9 apps 0 gls Total: 104 apps 1 gl

PRICE, James

Centre-half 5' 10½" 12st 2lbs
Born: Annbank, 24 April 1896
Died: Ashington, January quarter 1970
Career: Cumnock Juniors. Celtic August 1918. Dumbarton (loan) January 1919. Airdreonians June 1921. Nelson January 1922. ASHINGTON March 1923. North Shields May 1930. ASHINGTON December 1930. Wallaw United player and trainer August 1931. ASHINGTON trainer August 1933.

Debut v Walsall (h) 17.3.23, won 3-0

A cousin of Hugh Watson (Celtic right-back 1901-06), Jimmy Price commenced at Parkhead as a promising centre-half and first crossed the border to join Nelson, midway through their first season in the Northern Section of Division Three. After appearing in 20 consecutive matches in his first season he was replaced in the championship winning side of 1922-23 by Ernie Braidwood, the former Oldham Athletic team mate of player manager David Wilson. He left Seedhill to join the Colliers before the title was clinched, and three goals in nine matches in the final months of the season was an excellent start to his Ashington career. This he continued, with great distinction, amassing 244 senior appearances during Football League days, later returning to Portland Park as trainer when his playing career ended.

Appearances: FL: 233 apps 10 gls FAC: 11 apps 0 gls Total: 244 apps 10 gls

PRIOR, Willam Dinsdale

Right-back 5' 10" 12st 1lb
Born: Choppington, 8 August 1895
Died: Ashington, 4 December 1985
Career: Blyth Spartans. Bedlington United. Stakeford United January 1922. Choppington. ASHINGTON May 1924 to cs 1925. Returned to ASHINGTON after a season's absence in August 1926, but was not registered to play in FL matches.

Debut v Crewe Alexandra (h) 21.2.25, drawn 1-1

Hailing from a family of notable footballers, his brothers were Jack, an outside-right with Sunderland, Grimsby Town and Mansfield Town (258 League appearances and 51 goals). George was a full-back with Sheffield Wednesday and Watford (211 appearances). By comparison, William managed only one League appearance when promoted from the reserves, as deputy for George Hamilton. A second spell at Portland Park was also spent in reserve ranks throughout.

Appearances: FL: 1 app 0 gls Total: 1 app 0 gls

RAINNIE, Alexander

Left-half 5' 10" 9st 10lbs
Born: Banff, Scotland, 22 June 1891
Died: Durham North East, April quarter 1965
Career: South Shields. Newcastle United May 1919. Darlington May 1920, fee £20. ASHINGTON August 1923 to June 1924.

Debut v Doncaster Rovers (h) 27.8.23, won 3-1

Alex Rainnie's modest League career commenced after the First World War, during which he had served as a chief petty officer in the Royal Navy. His season with Newcastle United featured just one senior outing, but his performances at reserve team level with Darlington led to his appearance for the North Eastern League Select X1 versus the Central League in season 1921-22. His season at Portland Park followed a familiar pattern. Selected as first reserve for the opening fixture of the 1923-24 season, which was a 4-0 defeat at Wrexham, he was drafted in two days later for the midweek home fixture against Doncaster Rovers, but then spent the remainder of the season in the reserve team.

Appearances: FL: 1 app 0 gls Total: 1 app 0 gls

RANDALL, James

Inside or Outside-left
5' 10"   10st 10lbs
Born: Guide Post, Northumberland, 12 December 1904
Died: Ashington, July 1995
Career: Ashington Colliery Welfare. Sleekburn Albion. Bedlington United cs 1924.

ASHINGTON June 1925. Bradford City October 1928, fee £500. Derby County May 1930. Bristol City May 1935. ASHINGTON June 1936. Crookhill Colliery (by September 1938). Ashington Colliery Welfare coach (by 1946)
Debut v Nelson (h) 31.8.25, won 5-1 (scored a hat-trick)
Ashington secured the former miner's signature in 1925 and in his first game for the club he scored three goals against Nelson. In the early stages of season 1928-29, Randall's form on the Colliers left wing was attracting the scouts to Portland Park. Despite a thumping 8-2 home defeat against Bradford City on October 13th, he had done enough to earn a move to Valley Parade in the same month. Bradford City paid £400 for his services, with a provision for a further £100 if they won promotion, which they did. He joined a club on the upgrade, who scored 128 League goals in winning the championship of the Northern Section, losing only one match after New Year's Day 1929. In two seasons at Valley Parade he netted 16 League and Cup goals in 63 matches before joining First Division Derby County in May 1930. Competition at the Baseball Ground was fierce, but it was the signing of 'Dally' Duncan in March 1932 that effectively ended Randall's chances of regular first team football. A season with Bristol City wound up his senior career, with impressive career aggregate figures of 252 League appearances and 51 goals. Approximately half of his totals came with the Colliers, who fielded him at inside-forward for a little over two seasons before finding his best position on the left wing.

Appearances: FL: 124 apps 31 gls FAC: 5 apps 2 gls Total: 129 apps 33 gls
Honours: Bradford City, Division Three North champions, 1929.

RELPH, William

Inside-forward   5' 8½"   10st 9lbs
Born: Morpeth, 26 January 1900
Died: Newcastle-on-Tyne, 26 July 1978
Career: Seaton Delaval. Blyth Spartans amateur February, professional May 1920. ASHINGTON June 1921. Brentford July 1924. Blyth Spartans September 1926. Morpeth Church Institute (by February 1931). Pegswood United August 1931. Morpeth Town (by January 1934).
Debut v Grimsby Town (a) 3.9.21, lost 1-6
Billy Relph made only odd appearances for the first team in his debut season but finished with a flourish, scoring against Wigan Borough in a 1-1 draw on April 1st, and following with two goals in the return fixture, one week later, in a 3-1 win. His first extended run of senior football commenced from midway through the following season. Described as plucky and with a good shot, he netted nine goals in 21 League matches,

operating at either inside-right or left with equal faculty. Despite appearing in only four matches in 1923-24 he scored two goals, and it occurs that his overall goal scoring record deserved more opportunities than he was given. A brother, Steve, had trials with Derby County in 1931.
Appearances: FL: 32 apps 14 gls FAC: 2 apps 0 gls Total: 34 apps 14 gls

RICHARDSON, Edward 'Eddie'

Outside-left   5' 9"   11st 6lbs
Born: Ushaw Moor, 4 July 1894
Died: Durham, October quarter 1960
Career: Easington Colliery Welfare. South Shields June 1919. Newcastle United August 1922. Easington Colliery. Huddersfield Town December 1923. Sheffield Wednesday September 1924, in part-exchange for Sid Binks. South Shields 1925. York City February 1926. Bradford City September 1926, fee £100. Easington Colliery Welfare October 1928. ASHINGTON 18th October 1928. Easington Colliery Welfare by March 1930. Whitburn 1932. Easington Colliery Welfare by April 1933.
Debut v Accrington Stanley (a) 20.10.28, won 1-0
Eddie Richardson's career was spent mainly at reserve team level until he joined Bradford City where, in two seasons, he totalled 53 League and Cup appearances and scored 13 goals. Earlier in his career, he made his League debut with South Shields against Grimsby Town in Division Two in April 1920 and completed 34 League appearances, scoring four goals. A move to Newcastle United brought just two League appearances, and he failed to reach double figures with either Huddersfield Town or Sheffield Wednesday. Arriving at Portland Park in October 1928 he made an immediate impact, starring in the 1-0 win against Accrington Stanley on his debut and following up by scoring twice against Hartlepools United in a 3-1 win on 27th October. Sadly, the side failed to register further back-to-back wins throughout the remainder of the season. The Colliers last Football League match, against Halifax Town on 27th April also proved to be Richardson's swansong in senior football. His career aggregate figures were 125 League matches and 19 goals.

Appearances: FL: 23 apps 5 gls FAC: 1 app 0 gls Total: 24 apps 5 gls

RICHARDSON, William

Right-back
5' 7½"   11st 0lbs
Born: Hebburn-on-Tyne, April quarter 1898
Career: Jarrow. Wallsend Town. Stockport County May 1921. Poole F.C. August 1926. ASHINGTON November 1927. Durham City January 1928. ASHINGTON August 1928. Craghead United. Crookhall Colliery Welfare November 1929.
Debut v Tranmere Rovers (h) 12.11.27, won 3-0
Billy Richardson starred as Stockport County's right full-back for five seasons. Totally reliable and consistent, he made 25 appearances in his first season and picked up a Third Division North championship medal, a fitting reward for his contribution in a defence that conceded only 21 goals in 38 league matches. He left Edgeley Park after being transfer listed at the close of the 1925-26 relegation season with an outstanding record of 159 League and six FA Cup appearances. A season with Poole F.C. (later Poole Town), their first in the Southern League, included a memorable run in the FA Cup competition that ended with a 3-1 defeat against First Division giants Everton at Goodison Park. A return to the North-East began with an initial sojourn at Portland Park, covering just two appearances, before he was pitched headlong into Durham City's battle for League survival. Despite his best efforts in 14 consecutive appearances, the Citizens failed to avoid the drop following an unsuccessful re-election application. A personal highlight for the seasoned defender occurred on 7th April 1928 when he scored his solitary senior goal, successfully converting a penalty award in a 3-2 win against Bradford City. Arriving for a second

spell with Ashington in late August 1928 – along with John Stephenson, also from Durham City – Richardson failed to hold down the right full-back position and found himself in the unhappy position of a second, and ultimately unsuccessful, relegation battle.

Appearances: FL: 12 apps 0 gls Total: 12 apps 0 gls

Honours: Stockport County, Division Three North champions, 1922.

RIDLEY, Ralph Henry

Goalkeeper   5' 10"   11st 3lbs
Born: Haltwhistle, 14 April 1904
Died: Hamsterley, June 1932
Career: Chopwell Institute. ASHINGTON July 1924. York City November 1929. Consett September 1932. Workington (trial) August 1934. Throckley Welfare October 1934. Usworth Colliery Welfare.
Debut v Wrexham (h) 20.12.24, won 2-0

Aside from season 1925-26, when the goalkeeping position remained firmly in the hands of the former Preston North End custodian, John Elliott, Ralph Ridley enjoyed lengthy spells of first team action. He had his first chance in the League side when replacing Tom Newton, following a 7-1 defeat at Bradford Park Avenue in December 1924, and seized his opportunity, retaining the position for 24 consecutive matches through to the end of the season. After a season spent in reserve, the 1926-27 campaign began badly when he suffered a fractured finger in the final practice match in late August. After sitting out the early weeks of the campaign he was back in the first team picture again when he replaced Elliott in a 3-0 win against Halifax Town on November 13th, he then retained the jersey through to the end of the campaign. On December 4th, his outstanding display in the 1-0 victory against Hartlepools United included a dramatic, 90th minute save from a penalty taken by G.W. Richardson. His final season of first team involvement, 1927-28, was spent vying with Bill Bradley and included a run of 24 consecutive League and Cup matches, commencing on the 15th of October.

Appearances: FL: 74 apps 0 gls FAC: 5 apps 0 gls Total: 79 apps 0 gls

RITCHIE, William

Outside-right   5' 8½"   11st 4lbs
Born: Carlisle, 3 January 1897
Died: Hahira, Lowndes, Georgia, USA, January 1987
Career: Carlisle Schoolboys. RFC Depot. Derby County amateur August, professional November 1919. Porth FC May 1921. Sittingbourne August 1922. Millwall May 1923. ASHINGTON July 1924. Barrow June 1925. Montreal Scottish June 1926. New Bedford Whalers October 1926. J & P Coats (Rhode Island) February 1927. Boston Wonder Workers September 1928. New Bedford Whalers September 1930. Boston Wonder Workers 1931.
Debut v Doncaster Rovers (a) 8.9.24, lost 3-7

Billy Ritchie commenced in League football with Derby County in Division One in September 1919. He began well, scoring the only goal of the game on his debut against Aston Villa at the Baseball Ground, but played in only three more first team matches for the Rams. After a spell in non-League football, during which he was a Welsh League championship winner with Porth in 1922, he joined Millwall but again failed to establish himself, playing in only three first team matches. His first extended run of senior action came with the Colliers, and despite a faltering start he appeared regularly from mid January and scored twice at Barrow on 17th January in a 3-2 defeat. In the close season, along with Albert Tubb (q.v.), he moved to Holker Street, and made 28 appearances and scored one goal in Barrow's colours, before emigrating to Canada, continuing his football career both there and in America.

Appearances: FL: 19 apps 3 gls Total: 19 apps 3 gls

ROBERTSON, Thomas Henry

Centre-forward
5' 9½" 11st 4lbs
Born: Gateshead, 6 August 1889
Died: Gateshead, April quarter 1950
Career: Wallsend Park Villa. Lincoln City May 1910 to cs 1911. Wallsend Park Villa. Cardiff City May 1913.
ASHINGTON July 1919 to cs 1926.
Debut v Durham City (a) 24.9.21, lost 0-1

Tom Robertson's career suffered an early setback when he fractured his kneecap in a Lincoln City reserve team match in December 1910. He had earlier scored on his first team debut in a 2-2 draw against Glossop. Sadly, he was hospitalised for a lengthy spell and it was some years before he resumed in senior football. He was quickly into his stride with Cardiff City, however, scoring twice on his debut at Coventry City in October 1913. In the same month his tally had risen to five goals in four appearances, but his bright start was not maintained and he faded from the first team picture, completing just eleven matches, despite scoring six goals. After the Great War and army service he resumed his football career with Ashington, initially operating in the North Eastern League for two seasons, prior to entry into the Northern Section of Division Three. Robertson made his Football League debut in the season's first Northern "Derby" at Durham City. Just before the interval, he came close to giving the Colliers the lead when he crashed the ball against the crossbar, but in a match of few opportunities Durham scored the only goal of the game. In 37 League and Cup matches during the season, Robertson scored 24 goals to lead the scoring list by a very wide margin. He was similarly successful in the following two seasons (17 goals in 1922-23 and 18 in 1923-24) he featured less regularly thereafter, but his valuable contribution to the Colliers over a very long period was marked by a benefit match at Portland Park on Monday, 20th April 1925. An eleven chosen by Wilf Low, the former Newcastle United and Scotland International half-back, attracted 4,000 spectators to Portland Park. All went home happy as Ashington won 4-3 and the beneficiary, Tom Robertson, scored two of Ashington's goals.

Appearances: FL: 149 apps 61 gls FAC: 12 apps 7 gls Total: 161 apps 68 gls

ROBINSON, Charles Alexandra

Outside-right
5' 10½" 11st 5lbs
Born: Pegswood, April quarter 1906
Career: Pegswood United. Amble February 1926. Stakeford United. ASHINGTON amateur August 1926. Bedlington United (loan) August 1927.
Blackpool May 1928. Exeter City May 1931. Gillingham July 1933. Accrington Stanley June 1935. Rochdale June 1936. Blyth Spartans July 1938.
Debut v New Brighton (a) 28.8.26, lost 0-4

A younger brother of the Hartlepools United forward W.A. Robinson, Charlie began in League football with the Colliers, initially as an inside-forward. After just six matches in his first season he was loaned out to Bedlington United but returned in mid season, by this time operating as a dashing right-winger with an eye for goal. In 23 consecutive matches from December 31st 1927 he scored five goals and his inviting crosses supplied much of the ammunition for centre-forward George Johnson's 24 League goals. Rather surprisingly, his career after leaving Portland Park was spent at wing half-back. Three seasons with Blackpool were spent almost exclusively at reserve level and two seasons with Exeter City were similarly unproductive. Two seasons with Gillingham afforded more opportunities, and with Accrington Stanley he established himself in mid season and went on to appear in every match but one before the end of the campaign. His League career ended at Rochdale, where he was unfortunate to suffer a broken leg, ironically sustained in a collision with one of his own team-mates. His career aggregate figures were 118 League matches and four goals. Off the field he was a pianist of above average ability.

Appearances: FL: 29 apps 5 gls Total: 29 apps 5 gls

ROBINSON, Ian H

Right-half
Born: Scotland
Career: Scottish Junior Football. ASHINGTON January 1922.
Debut v Walsall (h) 21.1.22, lost 2-3

Walsall's initial visit to Ashington found the Portland Park camp confronted by difficulties. At the last moment, Featherstone and Galloway were unable to play having contracted influenza. The Reserves had already departed to Bedlington and the only available players were half-backs Trewick and Ian Robinson, the latter a Scottish Junior who had only joined the Colliers in the previous week. The game got underway, thirty-seven minutes late due to Walsall's late arrival. On a snowy pitch, Ashington were three goals in arrears in a little over half an hour. Dargue pulled one back just before the interval, but on the re-start the Colliers spurned a great opportunity when Thompson failed to score from the spot after Robertson had been brought down in the area. Four minutes from time, Robertson scored from close range, but despite great efforts to obtain the equaliser, Walsall won the points by three goals to two. Robinson failed to impress in his single League appearance.

Appearances: FL: 1 app 0 gls Total: 1 app 0 gls

ROBSON, George Arnold

Right-back
5'8"   11st 7lbs
Born: Tynemouth, 22 April 1897
Died: Blyth, 12 March 1984
Career: Cambois United. Blyth Spartans March 1914. North Shields October

1915. Raith Rovers and St. Mirren during the WW1 period. South Shields December 1919. Southampton June 1926. ASHINGTON September 1927. Blyth Spartans October 1931.
Debut v Accrington Stanley (h) 24.9.27, drawn 1-1

At the commencement of season 1920-21, George Robson, brother of John William (q.v.), was one of 46 players signed by South Shields, the total included nine full-backs, with Cresswell and Maitland the most regular pairing. It was some time before the short but sturdy Robson featured regularly at senior level, his best seasonal return being 29 matches in 1924-25. A season with Southampton was spent entirely at reserve team level, and he played little in his first season with the Colliers but returned after a very lengthy period out on 19th January 1929. A scratch eleven showing numerous changes did well to win a point at New Brighton in a 1-1 draw, but they remained rooted to the foot of the table. The last of his 14 appearances during the season came in a 3-0 defeat in the final match of the season against Halifax Town. Under the headline "Unlucky to the last", the *Newcastle Journal* reported that the home side were unfortunate to loose the services of George Robson due to injury, early in the second half. Already one down, Ashington conceded two more, and two goal line clearances by Chipperfield, when goals seemed certain, saved a heavier defeat. The game was watched by the lowest crowd of the season, only 706 spectators witnessing the Colliers swansong in the Football League.

Appearances: FL: 21 apps 0 gls Total: 21 apps 0 gls

Honours: St Mirren: Scottish Victory Cup winners 1919-20.

ROBSON, John William

Centre-forward   5'8½"   10st 8lbs
Born: Ashington
Career: Bedlington United. ASHINGTON amateur November 1924. Silkswood Colliery. ASHINGTON cs 1926. Silksworth Colliery January 1929. Blyth Spartans January 1931. Pegswood United 1931. ASHINGTON (trial) September 1931. Blyth Spartans October 1931. Bedlington United July 1933. Pegswood

United July 1934. Newbiggin West End April 1936. Ashington Committee December 1947.
Debut v Hartlepools United (h) 22.11.24, lost 0-3

At either centre-forward or inside-right "Butcher" Robson, as he was popularly known, often shone in reserve ranks but failed to rise to the occasion in infrequent first team appearances. He was still considered a reserve team player when he deputised for Harris – injured at Southport – in the first home match of 1928-29. A goal in the 4-2 win against Darlington got his season off to a good start, and an extended run of twelve matches from November onwards peaked on New Year's Day 1929, when he recorded a hat trick in the 3-2 win against Nelson at Portland Park. Surprisingly, he was released in the same month to return to Silksworth Colliery. As the Colliers, from that point on, won only two of their remaining seventeen League fixtures, it occurs that Robson's departure was extremely ill timed.
Appearances: FL: 24 apps 10 gls FAC: 1 app 0 gls Total: 25 apps 10 gls

ROBSON, Thomas

Outside-left
5' 7½"" 10st 12lbs
Born: Gosforth, Newcastle-on-Tyne
Career: Gosforth. Bedlington United. ASHINGTON pre-League (In Football League registrations he is said to be a retained player for season 1921-22). Durham City amateur December 1925. Carlisle United June 1928
Debut v Nelson (h) 14.10.22, lost 0-2

Tommy Robson made his Football League debut, and only appearance, against champions elect, Nelson in October 1922. He did rather better with Durham City, but had made little real progress until his third season at Holiday Park, when an enforced move to inside-forward, to allow an injured player to resume on the left wing, saw him

score twice against Rochdale in a 3-2 win. He ended the season with 30 appearances and five goals, but with League status lost following an unsuccessful re-election application, Robson moved on to Carlisle United, the team who replaced Durham City in the Third Division North.
Appearances: FL: 1 app 0 gls Total: 1 app 0 gls

SCOTT, Walter James

Right-half
Born: Willington Quay, 7 January 1890
Died: St Giles, Edinburgh, 10 November 1973
Career: Bedlington United. Heart of Midlothian March 1913, fee £50. Raith Rovers September 1915, also assisted St Bernard's, Dunfermline, Broxburn United and Falkirk during the WW1 period. Trials with Blyth Spartans and South Shields in August 1919. Hartlepools United August 1919 to April 1920.Blyth Spartans September 1920, fee £15. South Shields April 1921, fee £75. Close Works (Gateshead). ASHINGTON April 1922. Seaton Delaval October 1922. New Delaval Villa January 1924. Bebside Gordon September 1924. Coaching appointment in New Zealand 1928. Edinburgh City coach October 1932. Heart of Midlothian, Former Players' Association Committee and also scout to February 1937.
Debut v Hartlepools United (a) 15.4.22, lost 1-2

Of Scottish parentage, Walter Scott spent his best years in Scottish football, mainly with Heart of Midlothian. A reserve half-back for two seasons, he broke into the first team in 1914-15, the season in which the Tynecastle club saw thirteen of their players enlist in a new battalion being promoted in Edinburgh by Lieutenant-Colonel Sir George McCrae. In post war football Scott's only Football League appearances were made with South Shields (three matches), his single appearance with the Colliers being his last in senior football.
Appearances: FL: 1 app 0 gls Total: 1 app 0 gls
Honours: Heart of Midlothian: East of Scotland Shield 1914. Rosebery Charity Cup 1914. Dunedin Cup 1915 and Wilson Cup 1915.

SHEPHERD, John William Veitch

Goalkeeper
5' 9"   11st 4lbs
Born: Sunderland
Career: Stanhope Road School. Harton Colliery 1911. Jarrow 1913. Army football from 1915. Wartime guest player with Newcastle United 1918. Newcastle Swifts (briefly). Jarrow 1919. ASHINGTON July 1921. Luton Town August 1923. Workington February 1924. West Stanley June 1924 to cs 1927.
Debut v Wrexham (a) 10.9.21, lost 0-2
Prior to joining the Army in 1915, Shepherd had spent two seasons with Jarrow in the North-Eastern League. During military service in France he represented both his Brigade and Division, and was in goal for the eleven that won the Etaples League and medals. Two seasons with Jarrow preceded his move to Portland Park and throughout a similar period he contested the first team role with Alex Davidson. Although on the short side for his position he was said to deal equally well with high and low shots, and had a good command of his area. After leaving Ashington he spent seven months with Luton Town but appeared in only three Southern Section matches.
Appearances: FL: 41 apps 0 gls FAC: 1 app 0 gls Total: 42 apps 0 gls

SMITH, John

Right-half
Career: Leadgate Park. ASHINGTON amateur October 1921.
Debut v Barrow (h) 15.10.21, lost 0-2
Ashington made four changes in their team, two positional, for the visit of Barrow in the return fixture at Portland Park, but a crowd of 5,000 were greatly disappointed by the mediocre display of the Colliers, who were deservedly beaten by two clear goals. The home side's misfortune in losing Smith to an ankle injury, just three minutes into his debut in League football, was a bitter disappointment as he was unable to return and probably qualifies for the shortest Football League career on record. As the local correspondent ruefully noted: "Thereafter, Ashington rarely looked like rising to the occasion".
Appearances: FL: 1 app 0 gls Total: 1 app 0 gls

SOULSBY, James "John"

Inside or Outside-right
5' 8"   11st 2lbs
Born: Gateshead, October quarter 1896
Career: Gateshead Institute. Gateshead Rodsley. West Stanley April 1914. Newcastle United amateur May 1914. South Shields amateur December 1919. Darlington amateur July 1920. Blyth Spartans amateur May, professional September 1921. ASHINGTON July 1922. Blyth Spartans June 1923. Whitburn 1923. Spennymoor United November 1923. Carlisle United June 1924. Ravensworth Albion. Chester-le-Street Secondary Old Boys October 1928.
Debut v Wigan Borough (a) 26.8.22, lost 1-6 (scored)
A talented amateur, Soulsby was associated with Newcastle United as a teenager, but was without League experience when he joined the Colliers from Blyth Spartans in July 1922. A loss of £1,277 in the previous season had necessitated considerable pruning of expenses, but several new signings included Soulsby, who was expected to do well in a higher grade of football. On his debut at Wigan Borough, Ashington's new front line, with three new players, were said to move the ball around nicely, but they found Wigan's defence a stumbling block, Hunter the ex-Spurs goalkeeper and Currie ex-Leicester City being particularly effective. Soulsby scored the Colliers' only goal and held his place in the side for most of the season, switching from inside to outside-right in mid term. A schoolteacher by profession, Soulsby

returned to non-League football after his season with the Colliers.

Appearances: FL: 32 apps 6 gls FAC: 1 app 1 gl Total: 33 apps 7 gls

Note: Although he is named as "Jas." (short for James) in FL registrations, the family announcement of his death gave his forename as John.

STEPHENSON, John

Full-back   5' 8½"   12st 6lbs
Born: Croxdale, County Durham, January quarter 1896
Career: Croxdale F.C. Horden Athletic. South Shields (trial). Luton Town trial August, professional October 1921. Kettering Town January 1923. Durham City August 1924. Rochdale December 1927. ASHINGTON July 1928 to May 1929.
Debut v Southport (a) 25.8.28, lost 1-2
A late August 1928 report in the *Newcastle Journal* considered that Ashington's problem in the coming season would be largely financial. They had lost £1,450 in the previous season and with unemployment still rife in the district and the staple mining industry only working indifferently, the outlook was far from bright. Under the circumstances, the signing of players was delayed until the last minute, and three of the newcomers, including John Stephenson, had only been definitely fixed up in the week prior to the season's opener at Southport. His late arrival on the scene did not adversely affect the form of hefty full-back. Possessing all the qualities needed for successful defensive play and with the experience of in excess of 150 League appearances, he slotted seamlessly into the Colliers back division and was the only player with an ever-present record in what proved to be the Colliers swansong as a Football League club.
Appearances: FL: 42 apps 1 gl FAC: 1 app 0 gls Total: 43 apps 1 gl

STEVENS, John 'Jack'

Centre-half
5' 10"   11st 2lbs
Born: Morpeth, 1 February 1909
Died: Stockport, 2 December 1994
Career: Broomhill School. Northumberland Schoolboys. ASHINGTON November 1927. Bangor City (trial) September 1929. Middlewich October 1929. Manchester City December 1929, fee £250. Ashton National November 1930. Yeovil & Petters United June 1932. Stockport County September 1932. Brighton & Hove Albion June 1934 to 1939, continuing in wartime season 1939-40. Wartime guest player with Stockport County.
Debut v Accrington Stanley (h) 2.3.29, drawn 2-2
Jack Stevens won his County football cap as a schoolboy and was the winner of a £70 prize and gold medal when he won the Morpeth Spring Handicap. He made his Football League debut in the month following his 20th birthday, in what proved to be Ashington's last season as a Football League club. Later in the same year he joined Manchester City but failed to reach first team level, his first experience of regular football coming with Stockport County (66 League matches).

Moving to Brighton and Hove Albion in June 1934 he began at right-back but when switched to centre-half he retained the position for three seasons. In addition to his 137 League and 10 FA Cup appearances, Stevens made a further 38 appearances in wartime football before joining the Manchester Police Force.

Appearances: FL: 2 apps 0 gls Total: 2 apps 0 gls

TAIT, James Fordyce "John"

Inside-left
Born: Newcastle-on-Tyne, October quarter 1896
Died: Newcastle-on-Tyne, 4 October 1934, age 38
Career: Lintz Institute. ASHINGTON November 1919. Scotswood. Newcastle United May 1921. Lintz Intstitute 1922. ASHINGTON August 1922.
Debut v Wigan Borough (h) 2.9.22, won 2-1
An Ashington eleven with six new players never found their stride in the season's opener at Wigan Borough and were soundly beaten 6-1. Unsurprisingly, for the return fixture at Portland Park, the team was radically altered with three players, including Tait, making their debuts. The former Linz Institute forward worked hard on his first appearance but had little luck in front of goal. Early in the second half he netted but the point was disallowed as Robertson was adjudged off-side. A few minutes later he struck the upright and then shot just inches wide of the post. In the 2-1 win, the *Newcastle Journal* considered that Tait and McCloud had made a fine left wing, but the pairing was not persevered with. After a run of five matches, a series of changes at inside-left first saw Nichol Davidson, and later Billy Relph, the favoured selections.

Appearances: FL: 8 apps 1 gl FAC: 1 app 0 gls Total: 9 apps 1 gl
Note: Although named James in FL registrations, he was more commonly known as John, his father's forename.

TAYLOR, Albert

Outside-left   5' 10"   11st 9lbs
Born: Ashington, 10 July 1908
Died: Willesden, 28 December 1957

Career: Northumberland   County. ASHINGTON amateur September 1928. Armstrong Whitworth. Blyth Spartans January 1928. Bedlington United June 1929. South Shields amateur October 1929, professional December 1929. Chelsea May 1931, fee £500. Bristol Rovers May 1933. Lincoln City August 1936. Gillingham June 1937. Bexley Heath 1938. Welling United
Debut v Crewe Alexandra (h) 12.1.29, lost 0-5
In a career that eventually totalled 113 League appearances and 30 goals for six different clubs, Albert Taylor's baptism in League football was not a happy one. His single appearance for the Colliers resulted in a "rare drubbing" according to the local correspondent, who also considered that Taylor was not a success on his debut, being very erratic in the placing of his centres. After a spell in non-league circles, Taylor's career took an upturn with South Shields and Gateshead, who sold him to Chelsea in 1931. He did not fulfil expectations at Stamford Bridge, but enjoyed a productive spell with Bristol Rovers. Switched from the wing to centre-forward he netted 15 goals in 26 League matches in his first season, additionally assisting his team to win the Third Division South Cup against Watford in April 1935. In the following season his hat-trick in the 4-1 win against Oldham Athletic in the FA Cup third round replay at Eastville earned his side a plum fourth round home tie against Arsenal, the eventual winners of the trophy. A crowd of 24,234 packed into Eastville, but went home disappointed. Despite leading 1-0 at the interval the Rovers were well beaten, the Gunners winning 5-1 en route to Wembley and a 1-0 victory against Sheffield United. A season with Lincoln City (1936-37) was spent largely at reserve level, but his 19 Midland League goals placed him at the head of the scoring charts. Albert Taylor's League career wound up with Gillingham, and while he must have been delighted to score against his old club, Bristol Rovers, in his final outing, Gillingham finished the 1937-38 season at the foot of Division Three South and failed to gain re-election.

Appearances: FL: 1 app 0 gls Total: 1 app 0 gls
Honours: Bristol Rovers, Third Division South Cup winners, 1934.

TAYLOR, George

Inside-right   5' 8½"   11st lbs
Born: Cramlington
Career: Bedlington United. ASHINGTON
June 1921. Craghead United September 1924.
Cramlington Rovers August 1926.
Debut v Walsall (a) 28.1.22, lost 2-6
In August 1921 the *Athletic News* suggested
that Taylor, centre-half last season of the
North-Eastern League club Bedlington
United, would require consideration in the
Colliers' defence. In the event, he waited
until mid season for his League debut, and in
the unfamiliar role of left full-back he did not
have an happy baptism in the heavy defeat at
Walsall. In the final month of the season,
when eight League matches were contested,
Taylor was drafted in at inside-right and
scored the season's final goal in a 2-2 draw
against Southport. Retained for a further
season, he played in only two first team
matches before being released, returning to
local non-League football.
Appearances: FL: 7 apps 1 gl Total: 7 apps 1
gl

THIRWELL, Thomas William

Right-half
Born: Ashington, 4 April 1904
Died: Cramlington, 23 July 1969
Career: West Sleekburn. ASHINGTON
amateur August, professional September
1928. Cambois Welfare October 1930.
Debut v Southport (a) 25.8.28, lost 1-2
For the opening six fixtures of the 1928-29
campaign, local product Tom Thirwell
partnered Jimmy Price and Arthur Dalkin in
the Colliers' middle line. Although two of the
first three matches were won, defensive
frailties were blamed for defeats at New
Brighton and Stockport County and Thirwell
lost his first team spot and failed to regain it
in the Colliers' final season of League
football.
Appearances: FL: 6 apps 0 gls Total: 6 apps 0
gls

THOMPSON, George

Right-back
5' 10"   11st
7lbs
Born: Ashington
January quarter
1891
Career:
Bedlington
United. Burnley
April 1914.
Rotherham
County May
1921.

ASHINGTON January 1924. Pegswood
United 1926. ASHINGTON July 1928,
subsequently appointed trainer-coach.
Debut v Rochdale (a) 19.1.24, lost 0-1
Recruited by Burnley from Bedlington
United of the Northern Alliance in the season
preceding the Great War, centre-half George
Thompson had to wait until after the
hostilities before making his League debut.
As understudy to the Clarets' celebrated
captain Tommy Boyle, Thompson was
restricted to just five First Division
appearances in 1919-20 when Burnley
finished runners-up for the Championship. A
move to Second Division Rotherham County
brought more opportunities but, in his
second season, 1922-23, they lost their
Division Two place by the narrow margin of
just one point. Halfway through the following
season Thompson, by this time operating as
a right full-back, joined the Colliers. His
arrival immediately tightened the defensive
lines, enabling the side to finish eighth in the
table. In the following season he was
switched to right-half in mid term and it was
in this position that he saw out the 1925-26
campaign before leaving to join Pegswood
United at the age of 35. Returning to
Portland Park some two years later, his
duties including those of trainer-coach, he
made a final, emergency, appearance
towards the close of the campaign in a 3-1
defeat at Lincoln City.
Appearances: FL: 60 apps 2 gls FAC: 4 apps
0 gls Total: 64 apps 2 gls

THOMPSON, Robert

Centre-forward   6' 0"   12st 4lbs
Born: Eldon, County Durham
Career: Evenwood Juniors. Hartlepools United January 1919. Durham City August 1919. Leeds United May 1920. ASHINGTON May 1921. Luton Town June 1922. Pontypridd cs 1923. Accrington Stanley June 1924. Bury May 1925. Tranmere Rovers (trial) August 1926. Hartlepools United October 1926. Goole Town (trial) January 1927. York City January 1927.
Debut v Grimsby Town (h) 27.8.21, won 1-0
A former Powderhall sprint winner, Bob Thompson sampled almost every grade of football throughout a career spanning eleven clubs, and 40 goals in 95 matches for six different Football League teams. He was the first Leeds United player to score a hat-trick in League football, his treble coming against Notts County at Elland Road on 11th December 1920 in a 3-0 win. He finished the season as leading scorer with 12 League and Cup goals. Two second-half goals in the pre-season practice match at Portland Park – said to have attracted some 5,000 spectators – was a promising start for the former Leeds United centre-forward, and he scored two goals in his first four League matches. When Tom Robertson regained fitness, however, the previous season's leading scorer was reinstated as attack leader, Thompson switching to outside-right, a position eventually dominated by Jackie Foster. A season with Luton Town, during which he netted seven goals in 17 appearances, was followed by a record-breaking season with Pontypridd when he scored 51 goals and was selected to represent the Welsh League. His reputation as a goal scorer was upheld in a season with Accrington Stanley, his 17 goals in 33 matches including a hat-trick against Durham City in a 6-0 win. It was the first time that Stanley had scored six goals in a League match, but adverse weather conditions kept the attendance down to 500, with all-time low gate receipts of £22. A single appearance for Bury and three goals in four matches for Hartlepools United wound up his career in senior football.
Appearances: FL: 17 apps 2 gls FAC: 4 apps 1 gl Total: 21 apps 3 gls

Representative Honour: Welsh League v Free State League at Dalymount Park, Dublin, 9th February 1924.

TREWICK, Henry

Centre-half
Born: Tanfield, County Durham, 14 May 1898
Died: Karori, Wellington, New Zealand, 12 August 1966
Career: Scotswood amateur. Tanfield Lea Institute. ASHINGTON December 1921.
Debut v Nelson (a) 14.1.22, won 2-0
Reserve centre-half Henry Trewick found few opportunities at senior level during his spell at Portland Park being third in line behind experienced campaigners Pat O'Connell and Frank Knowles. His two League appearances were made consecutively, although he was fielded out of position on his home debut against Walsall. This came about when selected players Featherstone and Galloway were late withdrawals, both having contracted influenza. Trewick was pressed into service at inside-right and despite working hard, he never acclimatised to the unfamiliar position.
Appearances: FL: 2 apps 0 gls Total: 2 apps 0 gls

TUBB, Albert Ernest

Right-half
5' 9½"   11st 10lbs
Born: Eston, 24 July 1893
Died: Chesterfield, 17 February 1978
Career: South Bank January 1914. Normanby Magnesite. Yorkshire Amateurs. South Bank 1922.
ASHINGTON amateur March, professional July 1923. Barrow June 1925. Boston Town July 1926. Shirebrook June 1927. Chesterfield player-coach July 1928. Mexborough Athletic August 1929 to February 1930.
Debut v Walsall (h) 17.3.23, won 3-0
Albert Tubb began with South Bank, and after serving as a sergeant in the Northumberland Fusiliers during the Great

War, he resumed his football career, reaching the FA Amateur Cup Final in 1922 before taking the professional ticket with Ashington a year later. After just five League appearances as an amateur in the closing months of 1922-23, he played regularly in the following season but was not re-engaged, moving to Barrow, along with William Ritchie (q.v.). Sadly, his season at Holker Street ended with the team at the foot of the table, and his 35 League and Cup appearances proved to be his last, apart from a solitary outing with Chesterfield, who signed him as reserve team player-coach. Albert's brother, Arthur, also signed an amateur form with Ashington in April 1923, but he did not graduate beyond reserve team level.

Appearances: FL: 36 apps 0 gls FAC: 4 apps 0 gls Total: 40 apps 0 gls
Honours: South Bank: FA Amateur Cup finalists v Bishop Auckland, April 1922.

TURNBULL, Henry Wilkinson

Inside-right
Born: Tynemouth, 31 December 1902
Died: Newbiggin-by-the-Sea, 12 June 1970
Career: Newbiggin West End. ASHINGTON trial August 1926, amateur October 1926, professional February 1927. Blyth Spartans (trial) July 1928, professional August 1928. Newbiggin West End October 1929. Bedlington United October 1929 (An illegal transfer). Blyth Spartans 1930. Newbiggin West End (by 1932).
Debut v Rochdale (h) 16.10.26, drawn 2-2 (scored one)

First noted in a midweek pre season practice match for local amateurs on 18th August 1926, Turnbull was signed as an amateur some two months later and promptly stepped up to make his Football League debut. At one stage holding a comfortable 2-0 lead at Portland Park, Rochdale were pegged back through a Ted Ferguson penalty and, two minutes from the finish, the debutant brought the scores level when he netted following a corner kick taken by George Johnson. From a footballing point of view, Rochdale were considered the much better combined force, while Ashington lacked cohesion in the front line. Despite his contribution in saving his side a point,

Turnbull returned to reserve team football. He was given a six-match run in the first team in September 1927 and despite scoring against Lincoln City and Accrington Stanley was again banished to reserve ranks for the remainder of the season.
Appearances: FL: 9 apps 3 gls Total: 9 apps 3 gls

TURNBULL, William

Outside-right
5' 6½" 10st 10lbs
Born: Blyth, 21 December 1900
Career: Blyth United. New Delaval Villa. Blyth Spartans (trial) August 1920. West Stanley October 1920. Cardiff City April 1922. Newport County June 1924. ASHINGTON July 1925. Manchester City March 1926, fee £650. Chesterfield July 1927. Brighton & Hove Albion May 1928. ASHINGTON July 1929. Blyth Spartans August 1930. Wallsend Town October 1931.
Debut v Wigan Borough (h) 29.8.25, drawn 3-3

Although the £650 transfer fee received by Ashington for Billy Turnbull from Manchester City seems modest enough by today's standards, it enabled the Colliers to show a modest profit on the season's workings, despite lessened attendances at Portland Park throughout 1925-26. He had commenced the season at outside-right before switching to centre-forward in mid term, and his form during the campaign was outstanding. A particular highlight being his scoring of three hat-tricks, within the space of four matches, spanning January and February 1926. Earlier in his career, Turnbull scored 28 goals for West Stanley before joining Cardiff City. The bantam weight forward played almost exclusively at reserve level with both Cardiff City and Newport County, but represented the Welsh League versus the Irish League in 1923-24, and scored 36 goals for Newport County Reserves in 1924-25. After leaving Portland Park for the first time, he did not feature in

Manchester City's League side, but scored 11 goals in 29 matches for Chesterfield. A season in reserve with Brighton (five League appearances) preceded a second spell with the Colliers, by this time operating outside of the Football League. Turnbull's final League appearances were made with Gateshead (11 matches) and, despite his light weigh build, all were made as right full-back. A son, also William, played for Blyth Spartans and Hartlepools United "A" Team.

Appearances: FL: 34 apps 18 gls FAC: 1 app 0 gls Total: 35 apps 18 gls

WALLS, Frank Brown

Centre-forward   5' 9½"   10st 11lbs
Born: Stanraer, 8 November 1901
Died: Irvine, 24 April 1966
Career: Stranraer. Newton Stewart. Larne April 1923. Hull City (trial) August 1923. Stranraer. ASHINGTON December 1926. Newcastle United March 1927. Larne cs 1927. Stranraer December 1927.
Debut v Southport (a) 18.12.26, lost 1-4
Frank Walls scored two of his team's three goals on his debut for the Irish League at Cliftonville, Belfast, but the opposing centre-forward, Airdrieonians' Hughie Gallacher, did even better, scoring five of his team's seven goals in reply. In the following month, Newcastle United paid a club record fee of £6,500 to sign the celebrated Scottish international, whose career eventually spanned 624 senior matches and 463 goals. Frank Walls eventually reached Newcastle United, via Portland Park, but his stay was brief and he did not feature at senior level. Goals from the centre-forward position were very much at a premium throughout Ashington's 1926-27 season, Walls being goal-less in eight matches, but his late-season replacement as attack leader, Sam Ball, scored 10 goals in 12 matches to ease the side clear of the foot of the table.

Appearances: FL: 8 apps 0 gls Total: 8 apps 0 gls

Representative Honour: Irish League v Scottish League November 1925.

WARD, Edward

Inside-right
5' 6½"   11st 8lbs
Born: Cowpen, 16 June 1896
Career: Blyth Shamrocks. Blyth Spartans April 1913. Bedlington United June 1913. Blyth Spartans August 1919. Newcastle United May 1920, fee £300. Crystal Palace June 1922, fee £250. Nelson July 1923. Darlington (trial) November, professional December 1924. ASHINGTON August 1925. Workington August 1927. West Stanley August 1928. Carlisle United. Blyth Spartans player-coach October 1930, trainer August 1931, and still there in 1937.
Debut v Wigan Borough (h) 29.8.25, drawn 3-3 (scored two)
Spotted by Newcastle United when playing in a local cup final against the Magpies' reserve team, Ted Ward enjoyed some lengthy spells of first team football during season 1920-21, in which Newcastle challenged for the League Championship but ended the season in fifth place. A persistent knee injury blighted his spell with Crystal Palace, leading to his release on a free transfer after appearing in only four matches. He did little of note until he joined Ashington, where his brother Walter had assisted the reserve team two years earlier. Two goals on his debut got his Ashington career off to a bright start, and he was at his best in the opening weeks of the season as the Colliers took nine points from their first six League matches. It was, however, a sound defence that maintained the team in the top half of the League table for much of the season. In late August 1926, the *Athletic News* reported that Ward would not be seen in Ashington's colours in the forthcoming season. In the event, he was retained but spent much of the season in the reserve team who operated in the newly formed Second Division of the North-Eastern League, following the amalgamation with the Northern Alliance League.

Appearances: FL: 25 apps 10 gls FAC: 1 app 0 gls Total: 26 apps 10 gls

WATSON, William Thomas

Inside or Outside-left
5' 8"   10st 12lbs
Born: Cambais, 16 March 1899
Died: Littleborough, Lancashire, 5 April 1969
Career: Bolckow's United. Seaton Delaval. Blyth Spartans July 1922. ASHINGTON August 1923. Carlisle United June 1928. Rochdale August 1932. Accrington Stanley June 1933 to May 1934.
Debut v Wrexham (a) 25.8.23, lost 0-4

A fixture in the Colliers line-up, averaging 40 appearances per season in a five-year stay, only Jimmy Price, with 234 League outings, exceeded Billy Watson's 200 in the Colliers' colours. With a fine turn of speed and a trusty left foot the adaptable Watson could be relied upon for a full ninety minutes' display at either inside of outside left. Four seasons with Carlisle United followed, his spell at Brunton Park commencing with the Cumbrians' first fixture as a Football League club, won 3-2 at Accrington Stanley. His stay at Brunton Park ended with a flourish, his 17 goals in 31 matches included hat-tricks in both home and away fixtures against Doncaster Rovers. A season with Rochdale saw the durable wingman finish as joint leading scorer with 12 goals in 39 matches, half of his goals being scored within the space of six matches in December 1932. Although at the veteran stage when joining Accrington Stanley he completed 25 appearances, passing the milestone of 400 League appearances, all of which were played in the Northern Section of Division Three.
Appearances: FL: 200 apps 35 gls FAC: 12 apps 2 gls Total: 212 apps 37 gls

WILLIAMS, Thomas Hutchinson

Inside-forward
5' 9"   12st 0lbs
Born: Easington, 23 May 1899
Died: Easington, 14 December 1960
Career: Ryhope Colliery. Huddersfield Town (trial) February 1921. Clapton Orient August 1921. Charlton Athletic May 1923. Gillingham February 1924. ASHINGTON August 1924. Mid Rhondda August 1925. Bristol Rovers January 1926. Bristol City June 1928. Merthyr Town February 1929. Norwich City May 1930. Easington Colliery Welfare October 1933. Frost's Athletic August 1934.
Debut v Chesterfield (h) 30.8.24, won 2-1 (scored one).

One of the game's happy wanderers, the stocky and balding inside-forward began in League football with Clapton Orient, where he played alongside his brother, Owen, who was capped by England in 1923. Having scored on debut for both Charlton Athletic and Gillingham, Tom continued the sequence when he opened the scoring in Ashington's first fixture of season 1924-25, but he spent most of the season in reserve, with Billy Watson firmly established in the League side at inside-left. Subsequent successful spells with Bristol Rovers (27 goals in 75 matches) and Merthyr Town (19 goals in 43 matches) helped boost his final career aggregate figures to 81 goals in 218 League appearances. December 1960 brought double tragedy to the Williams family. Tom, aged 61, died just five days after his brother Owen had died, aged 65.
Appearances: FL: 10 apps 4 gls Total: 10 apps 4 gls

WILSON, Thomas

Right-half   5' 8"   11st 10lbs
Born: Cambois, Blyth
Career: Cambois Athletic. Shankhouse. Bradford Park Avenue (trial) 1927-28. Sheffield Wednesday (trial) March 1928. New Delaval Villa May 1928. ASHINGTON November 1928. Wallaw United November 1930. Blyth Spartans May 1931. Cambois Welfare August 1933. Morpeth Town August 1935.
Debut v Nelson (a) 8.12.28, lost 0-5
A brother of John Robert Wilson, a half-back with Portsmouth, Reading and Northampton Town who completed in excess of 200 League appearances in the 1920s. By comparison, Tom's career never reached the same heights, his only Football League appearances being those outlined below, in the Colliers final season as a Football League club.
Appearances: FL: 22 apps 0 gls Total: 22 apps 0 gls

NOTES ON THE APPEARANCE GRIDS

Home games are shown with the opponent's name in upper case. Ashington's score is always shown first.

League attendances to 1924-25 are as reported at the time. Those for 1925-26 onwards are official figures as recorded by the Football League. Some attendances prior to 1925 have not been found.

1921/22

10th in Division 3 (North)

#	Date		Opponent	Score	Scorers	Att	Barber JF	Beilby N	Bradford A	Brayson IH	Buxton S	Dargue T	Davidson A	Dickinson JH	Featherstone HW	Foster JTF	Galloway WM	Hamilton G	Hutchinson R	Knowles F	McCloud TE	McGill T	O'Connell P	Pigg W	Relph W	Robertson TH	Shepherd JW	Smith J	Taylor G	Thompson R	Trewick H
1	Aug	27	GRIMSBY TOWN	1-0	Dickinson	8000	6		2	11	3			8	4	7						10	5							9	
2	Sep	3	Grimsby Town	1-6	Thompson		6		2	11	3		1	8	4	7						10	5							9	
3		10	Wrexham	0-2		7000	6		2		3		1	8	4	7				11		10	5							9	
4		17	WREXHAM	2-2	McCloud, Thompson	7000			2		3	10	1	8	6	7				11			5							9	
5		24	Durham City	0-1		5000			2		3			6	7					8	5	11				10	1			9	
6	Oct	1	DURHAM CITY	1-0	Hutchinson	7000	6		2		3				7				8	4	11	10	5			9	1				
7		8	Barrow	0-2		7000	6		2		3				7				8	4	10	11	5			9	1				
8		15	BARROW	0-2		5000	6		2		3				7					5	11		8			9	1		4		
9		22	Crewe Alexandra	2-1	Robertson, Barber		10		2					3			8			4	11		5	6		9	1			7	
10		29	CREWE ALEXANDRA	0-1			10		2					3			8			4	11		5	6		9	1			7	
11	Nov	5	Lincoln City	1-4	Robertson				2					8	3					4	11	10	5	6		9	1			7	
12		12	LINCOLN CITY	4-2	Knowles, Robertson, Galloway, Dargue	5000			2			10	1		3		8			4	11		5	6		9				7	
13	Dec	24	CHESTERFIELD	1-0	Galloway	6000			2			10	1		3		8			4	11		5	6		9				7	
14		26	Tranmere Rovers	3-2	McCloud, Robertson, Dargue	8000	6		2			10	1		3		8			4			5			9				7	
15		27	Accrington Stanley	0-3		6000	4		2			10	1		7		3	8			5	11				9				7	
16		31	NELSON	4-0	Galloway, Dargue 2, Robertson	5000	4					3	10	1	2	7	8				11	5		6		9					
17	Jan	2	ACCRINGTON STANLEY	2-1	Knowles 2	5000	4		2			10	1		3	7	9			11	5			6	8						
18		3	Darlington	0-5		6000	4		2			10	1		2	7				5				8	6	11	9				
19		14	Nelson	2-0	Dargue, Featherstone (p)	3000					3	10	1		2	7	8			4	11			6		9					5
20		21	WALSALL	2-3	Dargue, Robertson	4000	2				3	10	1		2					5	11			6		9			7		8
21		28	Walsall	2-6	Robertson, O'Connell	7000	4					10	1		2	11							5	6	8	9			3	7	
22	Feb	4	HALIFAX TOWN	3-1	Dargue, Galloway, Featherstone (p)	1500		4	2			10			3	7	8				11		5	6		9	1				
23		11	Halifax Town	0-2		10000	4		2			10			3	7	8				11		5	6		9	1				
24		18	ROCHDALE	7-3	* See below	3000	10		2						3	8	7			4	11		5	6		9	1				
25		25	Rochdale	1-2	Robertson	3000	10		2						3	8	7		11	4			5	6		9	1				
26	Mar	4	TRANMERE ROVERS	1-0	Robertson	4200		4	2			10			3	8	7		11	5				6		9	1				
27		11	Southport	0-0		4000	10		2						4	8	7		11	5				6		9	1				
28		18	STALYBRIDGE CELTIC	2-3	Foster, Dargue	6000			2			3	10		4	8				5	11			6		9	1		7		
29		22	Chesterfield	1-0	Robertson	3000	10			11	3				2	8				4			5	6		9	1		7		
30		25	Stalybridge Celtic	0-2		4000	6				3				2	8		10		4	11		5			9	1		7		
31	Apr	1	Wigan Borough	1-1	Relph	7500			2			3	10		4	7				5	11			6	8	9	1				
32		5	DARLINGTON	1-0	Bradford (p)	6000			2			3			4	7			10	5	11			6	8	9	1				
33		8	WIGAN BOROUGH	3-1	Relph 2, Hutchinson	5000			2			3			4	7			10	5	11			6	8	9	1				
34		14	STOCKPORT COUNTY	2-0	Hutchinson 2	6000			2			3			4	7			10	5	11			6		9	1		8		
35		15	Hartlepools United	0-3		6000			2			3			4	7				5	11			6		9	1		8		
36		17	Stockport County	2-3	Robertson 2	14000	10		2			3			4	7				5	11			6		9	1		8		
37		22	HARTLEPOOLS UNITED	4-1	Robertson 3, Barber	2000	8		2			3			4	7			10	5	11			6		9	1				
38		29	SOUTHPORT	2-2	Robertson, Taylor	3000			2			3			4	7			10	5	11			6		9	1		8		
			Apps				23	2	31	2	24	15	12	3	31	30	11	1	22	34	28	6	19	29	7	33	26	1	5	17	2
			Goals				3					8	1		2	3	6			4	3	2	1		3	19			1	2	

Scorers in game 24: Galloway 2, Robertson 2, Foster 2, Barber

Played in one game: IRA Hine (game 5, at 4), J Henderson (8, at 10),
IH Robinson (20, at 4), W Scott (35, at 4)

F.A. Cup

Rnd	Date		Opponent	Score	Scorers	Att	Barber JF	Beilby N	Bradford A	Brayson IH	Buxton S	Dargue T	Davidson A	Dickinson JH	Featherstone HW	Foster JTF	Galloway WM	Hamilton G	Hutchinson R	Knowles F	McCloud TE	McGill T	O'Connell P	Pigg W	Relph W	Robertson TH	Shepherd JW	Smith J	Taylor G	Thompson R	Trewick H
Q4	Nov	19	CLOSE WORKS	6-0	* see below	2767			2				1		3	8				4	11	10	5	6		9			7		
Q5	Dec	3	LEADGATE PARK	2-1	Dargue 2	3670						10	1		3		8	2		4	11		5	6		9			7		
Q6		17	STALYBRIDGE CELTIC	1-0	Robertson	5785			2			10	1		3		8			4	11		5	6		9			7		
R1	Jan	7	Millwall	2-4	Robertson 2	20000			2			10	1		3		8			4	11		5	6		9			7		

Scorers in Q4: McGill 2, Foster, Robertson 2, Thompson

1922/23

19th in Division 3 (North)

#		Date	Opponent	Score	Scorers	Att	Archer GT	Bailey HA	Bradford A	Burton R	Collier J	Davidson A	Davidson NT	Draper JP	Featherstone HW	Foster JTF	Hall T	Hamilton G	Hunter N	Loughran T	Mahon P	McCloud TE	Morton J	Nicholson J	Pigg W	Price J	Relph W	Robertson TH	Shepherd JWV	Soulsby J	Tait JF	Taylor G	Tubb AE
1	Aug	26	Wigan Borough	1-6	Soulsby	7000			2	6						7	10				3	11	5		4			9		8			
2	Sep	2	WIGAN BOROUGH	2-1	McCloud, Robertson	5000	5				6				3	7					2	11			4			9	1	8	10		
3		9	Darlington	1-1	Foster	5000	5				6				3	7					2	11			4			9	1	8	10		
4		16	DARLINGTON	3-1	Robertson 2, Mahon (p)	7000	5				6				3	7					2	11			4			9	1	8	10		
5		23	Hartlepools United	1-3	Robertson	5000	5				6				3	7					2	11			4			8	1	9	10		
6		30	HARTLEPOOLS UNITED	4-2	Soulsby, Tait, Featherstone, Mahon(p)	6000	5				6				3	7					2	11			4			9	1	8	10		
7	Oct	7	Nelson	3-1	Soulsby, Robertson 2	7000			5	6					3	7					2	11			4			9	1	8		10	
8		14	NELSON	0-2		8000		3	5	6						7	10				2				4			9	1	8			
9		21	Chesterfield	2-2	Robertson, Soulsby	8000			5	6				10	3	7					2				4			9	1	8			
10		28	CHESTERFIELD	2-0	N Davidson, Robertson	6000			5	6				10	3	7					2	11			4			9	1	8			
11	Nov	4	Stalybridge Celtic	1-2	Mahon (p)	3000			5	6				10	3	7					2	11			4			9	1	8			
12		11	STALYBRIDGE CELTIC	0-3		6000			5	6				10	3	7					2	11			4			9	1	8			
13		18	Southport	0-1		5659	5			6				10	2	7		3				11			4			9	1	8			
14		25	SOUTHPORT	1-1	Robertson	5000			2	6				8	3	7						11			4			9	1	5	10		
15	Dec	9	LINCOLN CITY	0-2		3000			2	5	1			10	3	7									4	6		9		8		11	
16		23	BARROW	2-6	Robertson, Soulsby	3000	5	3		6					4	7					2		11			10		9	1	8			
17		25	Tranmere Rovers	0-1		7000			2	9	1			10	6	7					3	11			5	4		8					
18		26	Accrington Stanley	1-4	Burton	4000			2	9	1			10	6	7					3	11			5	4		8					
19		30	Rochdale	0-2		2000	4			6	1			10	3	7					2	11			5		8	9					
20	Jan	1	DURHAM CITY	0-0		3000	4			6	1				3	11					2				5		8	9		7	10		
21		6	ROCHDALE	2-0	Relph 2	4000				6	1			10	3	11					2				5		8	9		7			
22		13	Barrow	0-3		3000				6	1			10	3	11					2				5		8	9		7			
23		20	WREXHAM	1-1	Relph	4000				6	1	9			2	11			3	5							8	10		7			
24		27	Wrexham	0-0		5000				6	1	9			3	11				5				2	4		8	10		7			
25	Feb	3	Crewe Alexandra	1-3	McCloud	5000				6	1	9			3	11				5		7		2	4		8	10		7			
26		10	CREWE ALEXANDRA	2-4	Pigg, Robertson	1500				6	1	10			3	11				5		7		2	4		8	9					
27		17	GRIMSBY TOWN	2-1	Draper, Robertson	2000					1	6		9	2	11			3	5					4		8	10		7			
28		24	Grimsby Town	4-7	* See below	4000					1	6		9	2	11			3	5					4		8	10		7			
29	Mar	3	ACCRINGTON STANLEY	2-5	Robertson 2	3500					1	6			2	11			3	5					4		8	9		7			10
30		17	WALSALL	3-0	Hunter, Robertson, Relph	4646				6	1				2	11			3	8					5		10	9		7			4
31		24	Walsall	1-2	Foster	8000				4	1				2	11			3	8					5		10	9		7			6
32		30	Lincoln City	0-2			4			6	1	3			2	11		8							5		10	9		7			
33		31	HALIFAX TOWN	3-2	Price, Robertson, Relph	4000	4			6	1	3			2	11		8							5		10	9		7			
34	Apr	2	Durham City	1-1	Price	2000	4			6	1	3			2	11		8							5		10	9		7			
35		7	Halifax Town	0-0		4000				6	1				2	11		8						3	5	4	10	9		7			
36		14	BRADFORD PARK AVE.	2-1	Relph 2	4000				6	1	3			2	11		8							5		10	9		7			4
37		21	Bradford Park Avenue	0-3		10000				6	1	3			2	11		8							5		10	9		7			4
38		28	TRANMERE ROVERS	3-1	Price, Relph, Soulsby	3000			3	6					2	11		8							5		10	9		7			4
			Apps				11	2	7	29	17	23	13	5	35	38	2	7	9	7	24	17	9	3	26	9	21	38	15	32	8	2	5
			Goals										1	1	1	2			1		1	3	2			1	3	9	17		6	1		

Scorers in game 28: Relph, Coupland (og), Robertson, Bradford (og)

Played in one game: T Robson (game 8, at 11), M Goonan (9, at 11), J Bainbridge (37, at 7), R Morton (16, at 11)

Two own goals

F.A. Cup

#		Date	Opponent	Score	Scorers	Att	Archer GT	Bailey HA	Bradford A	Burton R	Collier J	Davidson A	Davidson NT	Draper JP	Featherstone HW	Foster JTF	Hall T	Hamilton G	Hunter N	Loughran T	Mahon P	McCloud TE	Morton J	Nicholson J	Pigg W	Price J	Relph W	Robertson TH	Shepherd JWV	Soulsby J	Tait JF	Taylor G	Tubb AE
Q5	Dec	2	Blyth Spartans	1-2	Soulsby	8000			5	4					2	7					3	11			6			9	1	8	10		

1923/24

8th in Division Three (North)

#		Date	Opponent	Score	Scorers	Att	Chipperfield F	Coutts T	Davidson A	Gardner W	Griffiths T	Hamilton G	Henderson T	Hepple R	Hoffman EH	Kidd E	Laverick W	Page G	Pigg W	Price J	Rainnie A	Relph W	Robertson TH	Thompson G	Tubb AE	Watson WT
1	Aug	25	Wrexham	0-4		6000	2			10	9		6		1		7	11	3	5					4	8
2		27	DONCASTER ROVERS	3-1	Watson, Price, Gardner	6000			1	10			2				7	11	3	5	6		9		4	8
3	Sep	1	WREXHAM	0-2		6300			1	8			2				7	11	3	6	5		9		4	10
4		3	Doncaster Rovers	1-2	Page (p)	7000	5		1	8			2	7				11	3	6			9		4	10
5		8	Wigan Borough	1-1	Robertson	12000			1	8			2	7				11	3	6	5		9		4	10
6		15	WIGAN BOROUGH	3-0	Watson, Gardner 2	6000			1	8			2	7				11	3	6	5		9		4	10
7		29	DURHAM CITY	2-1	Gardner, Robertson	5800				8			2	7	1			11	3	6	5		9		4	10
8	Oct	6	Crewe Alexandra	3-1	Gardner 2, Robertson	5000				8			2	7	1			11	3	6	5		9		4	10
9		13	CREWE ALEXANDRA	3-0	Gardner 2, Robertson	5000				8			2	7	1			11	3	6	5		9		4	10
10		20	ACCRINGTON STANLEY	1-1	Gardner	5000				8			2	7	1			11	3	6	5		9		4	10
11		27	Accrington Stanley	1-0	Hepple	5000				8			2	7	1			11	3	6	5		9		4	10
12	Nov	3	HALIFAX TOWN	4-0	Watson, Robertson 2, Laverick	5000				8			2	7	1			11	3	6	5		9		4	10
13		10	Halifax Town	0-3						8			2	7	1			11	3	6	5		9		4	10
14		24	ROTHERHAM COUNTY	1-2	Gardner	5358				8			2		1			11	3	6	5		9	7	4	10
15	Dec	8	GRIMSBY TOWN	1-0	Relph					8			2		1			11	3	4	5	7	9		6	10
16		22	NEW BRIGHTON	5-0	Laverick 2, Page, Robertson, Gardner	4000				8			2		1	7	11	3	6	5			9		4	10
17		25	Tranmere Rovers	4-2	* see below	6000				10			2		1	11	7	3	4	5			9		6	8
18		26	New Brighton	1-1	Watson	6000				10			2		1	11	7	3	4	5			8		6	9
19		29	Wolverhampton Wan.	0-1		17000				7			2		1	10	11	3	6	5			8		4	9
20	Jan	1	WALSALL	3-1	Robertson 2, Gardner	6000	5			8			2		1	7	11	3					9		4	
21		5	WOLVERHAMPTON W.	1-7	Watson	8824				7			2		1	10	11	3	6	5			8		4	9
22		19	Rochdale	0-1		6000	5	4		8					1	7	11	3	6				9	2		10
23		26	ROCHDALE	1-0	Laverick	5400	5			9					1	7	11	3	6			8		2	4	10
24	Feb	2	Southport	0-2		5000				8					1	7	11	3	6	5			9	2	4	10
25		9	SOUTHPORT	2-0	Robertson 2	3500				8					1	7	11	3	6	5			9	2	4	10
26		16	Darlington	2-3	Relph, Robertson	5000				8					1	7	11	3	6	5		8	9	2	4	10
27		23	DARLINGTON	2-1	Gardner, Watson	5800	4			8					1	7	11	3	6	5			9	2		10
28	Mar	1	BARROW	2-0	Laverick, Robertson	5800	4			8					1	7	11	3	6	5			9	2		10
29		8	Barrow	2-2	Gardner 2 (1p)	3000	4			8					1	7	11	3	6	5			9	2		10
30		15	LINCOLN CITY	2-1	Gardner 2	3000				8					1	7	11	3	6	5			9	2	4	10
31		17	Rotherham County	0-1		7000	4			8					1	7		3	6	5			9	2	10	11
32		22	Lincoln City	0-2						8					1	7	11	3	6	5			9	2		10
33		29	TRANMERE ROVERS	3-3	Robertson 2, Watson	4568		7	1	8							11	3	6	5			9	2	4	10
34	Apr	5	Durham City	0-4		4000	3	7	1	8							11		6	5			9	2	4	10
35		8	Grimsby Town	0-4		4000	4			8	2				1	7	11	3	6	5			9			10
36		12	BRADFORD PARK AVE.	1-0	Robertson	2000	4			8					1	7	11	3	6	5			9	2		10
37		18	HARTLEPOOLS UNITED	0-0		6000	4			8	3				1	7	11		6	5			9	2		10
38		19	Bradford Park Avenue	1-3	Laverick	6000	4			8	3				1	7	11		6	5			9	2		10
39		21	Walsall	1-1	Robertson	3245	4			8		2			1	7	11	3	6				9	5		10
40		22	Hartlepools United	1-0	Gardner	2000	5			8	3				1	7	11		6	4			9	2		10
41		26	CHESTERFIELD	1-1	Robertson	4000	4			8	3				1	7	11		6	5			9	2		10
42	May	3	Chesterfield	0-2		4000	4			8	3				1	7	11		6	5			9	2		10

Scorers in game 17: Campbell (og), Laverick, Watson, Gardner

						Apps	16	5	7	41	1	6	22	10	35	28	41	36	40	37	1	4	40	20	30	42
						Goals				19			1				7	2		1		2	18			8

One own goal

F.A. Cup

		Date	Opponent	Score	Scorers	Att	Chipperfield F	Coutts T	Davidson A	Gardner W	Griffiths T	Hamilton G	Henderson T	Hepple R	Hoffman EH	Kidd E	Laverick W	Page G	Pigg W	Price J	Rainnie A	Relph W	Robertson TH	Thompson G	Tubb AE	Watson WT
Q4	Nov	17	Bishop Auckland	2-1	Gardner 2					8			2		1		11	3	6	5		7	9		4	10
Q5	Dec	1	CARLISLE UNITED	2-0	Laverick 2	4753				8			2		1		11	3	6	5		7	9		4	10
Q6		15	HARTLEPOOLS UNITED	2-1	Watson, Gardner	6540				8			2		1	7	11	3	6	5			9		4	10
R1	Jan	12	ASTON VILLA	1-5	Robertson	11837				8					1	7	11	3	6	5			9	2	4	10

66

1924/25

10th in Division Three (North)

#	Mon	Date	Opponent	Res	Scorers	Att	Alexandra JW	Anderson J	Chipperfield F	Cooper JW	Coutts T	Fenwick AR	Ferguson E	Gardner W	Guthrie GR	Hamilton G	Henderson T	Hodgson T	Johnson GA	Newton T	Laverick W	Morton R	Price J	Prior WD	Ridley RH	Ritchie W	Robertson TH	Robson JW	Thompson G	Tubb AE	Watson WT	Williams TH
1	Aug	30	CHESTERFIELD	2-1	Williams, Gardner	5000	7					5	2	8		3	6		1		4						9				11	10
2	Sep	1	DONCASTER ROVERS	2-0	Henderson, Williams	5000	7					5	2	8		3	6		1		4						9				11	10
3		3	Durham City	0-0		2000	7					5	2	8		3	6		1	11	4										10	9
4		6	Nelson	0-4		6000						5	2	8		3	6		1	11	4						9				10	7
5		8	Doncaster Rovers	3-7	Williams, Robertson, Gardner	6000						5	2	8		3	6		1		4				7		9				11	10
6		13	BARROW	5-2	* see below	4000	7					5	2	8		3	6		1	11	4						9				10	
7		16	Southport	0-3		4000	7		6				2	8		3	4		1	11	5						9				10	
8		20	Lincoln City	0-5		8000				6		5	2			3	4		1	11					7		9				10	8
9		27	TRANMERE ROVERS	1-0	Gardner	5000						5		8		3	6		1	11	4				7		9		2		10	
10	Oct	4	Walsall	0-1		7420	7					5		8		3	6		1	11	4						9		2		10	
11		11	Wigan Borough	0-2		8000						5		8		3	6		1	11	4				7		9		2		10	
12		18	Crewe Alexandra	0-1					6			5			1	3	9	8		11	4						10		2			7
13		25	ACCRINGTON STANLEY	1-2	Watson	4000					7	5		8	1	3	6			11	4						9		2		10	
14	Nov	1	Halifax Town	0-0		5000			6	7				8		3	4		1	11	5						9		2		10	
15		8	NEW BRIGHTON	1-1	Robertson	4000	7		6					8		3	4		1	11	5						9		2		10	
16		22	HARTLEPOOLS UNITED	0-3		4000		7	6					8		3	4		1	11	5								2	9		10
17	Dec	6	DARLINGTON	4-2	Watson, Henderson, Robson, Gardner	5800							6	8		3	4		1	11	5						9	7	2		10	
18		17	Bradford Park Avenue	1-7	Laverick	5000							6	8		3	4		1	11	5						9	7	2		10	
19		20	WREXHAM	2-0	Robertson, Hodgson	1311			6		4			8		3		9		11	5		1		7				2		10	
20		25	Rotherham County	4-1	Gardner 3, Hodgson				6		4			8		3		9		11	5		1		7				2		10	
21		27	Chesterfield	1-1	Johnson	4000			6		4			8		3			9	11	5		1		7				2		10	
22	Jan	1	ROTHERHAM COUNTY	3-1	Price, Gardner, Johnson	2000			6				2	8		3			9	11	5		1		7				4		10	
23		2	ROCHDALE	4-3	* see below	4000			6				2	8		3			9	11	5		1				7		4		10	
24		3	NELSON	1-1	Watson	4245			6				2	8		3			9	11	5		1				7		4		10	
25		10	Grimsby Town	3-1	Johnson, Gardner 2	6000			6				2	8		3			9	11	5		1			7			4		10	
26		17	Barrow	2-3	Ritchie 2	4000			6				2	8		3			9	11	5		1			7			4		10	
27		24	LINCOLN CITY	2-1	Johnson 2	3380			6				2	8		3			9	11	5		1			7			4		10	
28		31	Tranmere Rovers	4-5	Watson 3, Price	3000			6				2	8		3			9	11	5		1			7			4		10	
29	Feb	7	WALSALL	6-1	* see below	4000			6				2	8		3			9	11	5		1			7			4		10	
30		14	WIGAN BOROUGH	1-1	Laverick	3000			6				2	8		3			9	11	5		1			7			4		10	
31		21	CREWE ALEXANDRA	2-1	Johnson	4000			6					8		3			9	11	5	2	1			7			4		10	
32		28	Accrington Stanley	2-2	Gardner, Johnson	5000			6		4		2	8		3			9	11	5		1			7					10	
33	Mar	7	HALIFAX TOWN	2-0	Johnson, Ritchie	4000			6		4		2	8		3			9	11	5		1			7					10	
34		14	New Brighton	4-4	Laverick, Johnson 2, Williams	4000					4		2			3			9	11	5		1			7			6		10	8
35		21	GRIMSBY TOWN	0-2		3200			6				2	8		3			9	11	5		1			7			4		10	
36		28	Hartlepools United	1-0	Gardner	4000			6		4		2	8		3			9	11			1		7				5		10	
37	Apr	4	Rochdale	0-0		6000			6		4		2			3			9	11			1		7				5		10	8
38		10	DURHAM CITY	0-2		5000			6		4			8		3				7	11	5		1					2		10	9
39		11	Darlington	1-2	Greaves (og)	8000			6				2	8		3			9	11	5		1		7				4			10
40		18	BRADFORD PARK AVE.	1-0	Johnson	2000			6				2	8		3			9	11	5		1		7		10		4			
41		25	Wrexham	1-3	Laverick	6000			6				2	8		3			9	11	5		1		7		10		4		7	
42	May	2	SOUTHPORT	2-0	Johnson, Gardner	4000			6				2	8		3			9	11	5		1		7				4		10	

Scorers in game 6: Gardner 2, Watson, Robertson, Henderson
In game 23: Robertson, Johnson, Thompson, Gardner
In game 29: Gardner (p), Laverick, Thompson, Johnson 2, Watson

| | | | | | | Apps | 7 | 1 | 14 | 2 | 27 | 12 | 31 | 38 | 2 | 40 | 18 | 2 | 22 | 16 | 38 | 2 | 39 | 1 | 24 | 19 | 25 | 3 | 30 | 1 | 38 | 10 |
| | | | | | | Goals | | | | | | | | 17 | | | 3 | 2 | 15 | | 5 | | 2 | | 3 | 5 | 1 | | 2 | | 8 | 4 |

One own goal

F.A. Cup

							Alexandra JW	Anderson J	Chipperfield F	Cooper JW	Coutts T	Fenwick AR	Ferguson E	Gardner W	Guthrie GR	Hamilton G	Henderson T	Hodgson T	Johnson GA	Newton T	Laverick W	Morton R	Price J	Prior WD	Ridley RH	Ritchie W	Robertson TH	Robson JW	Thompson G	Tubb AE	Watson WT	Williams TH
Q4	Nov	15	Hartlepools United	0-0		5692			4		7			8		2	6		1	11	5						9		3			10
rep		19	HARTLEPOOLS UNITED	2-0	Gardner 2	4000	7		4					8		2	6		1	11	5						9		3			10

Ashington disqualified for fielding an ineligible player - John Anderson

67

1925/26

9th in Division 3 (North)

#	Date	Opponent	Result	Scorers	Att	Archer GT	Brannan F	Carlton J	Chester C	Chipperfield F	Cousins HD	Coutts T	Craig T	Crane JP	Dalkin JW	Elliott JW	Ferguson E	Gardner W	Hamilton G	Johnson GA	Price J	Randall J	Robertson TH	Thompson G	Turnbull WJ	Ward E	Watson WT
1	Aug 29	WIGAN BOROUGH	3-3	Johnson, Ward 2	4674							10		6		1	2		3	9	5				4	7	8 11
2	31	NELSON	5-1	Randall 3, Johnson, Turnbull	3902							6				1	2		3	9	5	10			4	7	8 11
3	Sep 5	New Brighton	1-1	Watson	6251				4			6				1	2		3	9	5	10				7	8 11
4	9	COVENTRY CITY	2-0	Johnson, Turnbull	4175					4		6				1	2		3	9	5	10				7	8 11
5	12	CREWE ALEXANDRA	2-0	Johnson 2	4659					4		6				1	2		3	9	5	10				7	8 11
6	15	Nelson	2-2	Johnson, Newnes (og)	7461				4			6				1	2		3	9	5	10				7	8 11
7	19	Lincoln City	0-2		3138				4			6				1	2		3	9	5	10				7	8 11
8	26	SOUTHPORT	1-1	Randall	4094	4						6				1	2	8	3	9	5					7	11
9	Oct 3	Doncaster Rovers	1-2	Randall	6517					6	4					1	2	9	3		5	10				7	8 11
10	10	WREXHAM	2-2	Randall, Gardner	4244					6	4					1	2	9	3	8	5	10				7	
11	17	Rochdale	3-1	Gardner, Randall, Turnbull	4089					6	4					1	2	9	3	8	5	10				7	
12	24	TRANMERE ROVERS	1-0	Watson	4499					6	4					1	2	9	3	8	5	10				7	
13	31	Accrington Stanley	1-2	Ward	4823					4	6					1	2		3	9	5	8				7	10 11
14	Nov 7	DURHAM CITY	0-1		3084					4	6					1	2		3	9	5					7	10 11
15	14	Bradford Park Avenue	0-1		12135			4	10	6						1	2		3	9	5					7	8 11
16	21	GRIMSBY TOWN	4-2	Ward 2, Turnbull, Johnson	4537	4	6			3						1	2			10	5			9	7	8 11
17	Dec 5	HALIFAX TOWN	0-1		2847			4		6						1	2		3	10	5			9	7	8 11
18	12	Walsall	0-2		1904			10		6						1	2		3	9	5				4	7	8 11
19	19	CHESTERFIELD	0-0		1646					6						1	2		3	9	5	8			7	10 11
20	25	BARROW	1-4	Cousins	3673					5	8	6				1	2		3	9			10		4	7	11
21	26	Hartlepools United	1-2	Robertson	5094			4		6	8					1	2		3	10	5		9		7		11
22	Jan 1	Barrow	3-2	Turnbull, Watson, Dalkin	2957					6	8				7	1	2		3	4	5		10		9		11
23	2	Wigan Borough	2-0	Dalkin, Carlton	4679			8		6					7	1	2		3	4	5		10		9		11
24	9	Halifax Town	0-0		9397			8		6					7	1	2		3	4	5		10		9		11
25	16	NEW BRIGHTON	1-1	Turnbull	3799			8		6					7	1	2		3	4	5				9		11
26	23	Crewe Alexandra	1-2	Dalkin	3783			8		6					7	1	2		3	4	5	10			9		11
27	30	LINCOLN CITY	4-1	Turnbull 3, Dalkin	3595			8	4	3					7	1			2	6	5	10			9		11
28	Feb 6	Southport	1-1	Dalkin	3777			8				4			7	1			3	6	5	10		2	9		11
29	13	DONCASTER ROVERS	6-1	Carlton, Randall, Watson, Turnbull 3	3778			8							7	1	2		3	6	5	10		4	9		11
30	20	Wrexham	3-2	Turnbull 3	5190			8							7	1	2		3	6	5	10		4	9		11
31	22	Rotherham United	1-5	Ferguson	3432			8							7	1	2		3	6	5	10		4	9		11
32	27	ROCHDALE	0-1		4270			8							7	1	2		3	6	5	10		4	9		11
33	Mar 6	Tranmere Rovers	4-1	Turnbull 2, Watson, Ward	5380					6					7	1	2		3	4	5	10			9	8	11
34	13	ACCRINGTON STANLEY	3-1	Watson, Turnbull, Ward	4353					6					7	1	2		3	4	5	10			9	8	11
35	20	Durham City	0-0		3090					6	8				7	1	2		3	4	5	9				10	11
36	27	BRADFORD PARK AVE.	1-1	Cousins	5517					6	8				7	1	2		3	4	5	10	9				11
37	Apr 2	HARTLEPOOLS UNITED	2-0	Cousins, Robertson	4596					6	8				7	1	2		3	4	5	10	9				11
38	3	Grimsby Town	1-3	Dalkin	10284					6	8				7	1	2		3	4	5	10	9				11
39	5	Coventry City	0-2		5073					6	7					1	2		3	4	5	10	9			8	11
40	10	ROTHERHAM UNITED	4-2	Chipperfield 2, Ward, Randall	2793					6					7	1	2		3	4	5	10	9			8	11
41	24	WALSALL	2-0	Randall, Watson	2588			8		6					7	1	2		3	4	5	10	9				11
42	May 1	Chesterfield	1-6	Carlton	2306			8		6				9	7	1	2		3	4	5	10					11

| | | | | | Apps | 1 | 4 | 18 | 4 | 31 | 8 | 14 | 1 | 1 | 20 | 42 | 40 | 5 | 41 | 41 | 32 | 13 | 9 | 34 | 20 | | 42 |
| | | | | | Goals | | 3 | 2 | | 3 | 6 | | | | | | 1 | 2 | | 7 | | 10 | 2 | | 18 | 8 | 7 |

One own goal

F.A. Cup

#	Date	Opponent	Result	Scorers	Att	Archer GT	Brannan F	Carlton J	Chester C	Chipperfield F	Cousins HD	Coutts T	Craig T	Crane JP	Dalkin JW	Elliott JW	Ferguson E	Gardner W	Hamilton G	Johnson GA	Price J	Randall J	Robertson TH	Thompson G	Turnbull WJ	Ward E	Watson WT
R1	Dec 2	Durham City	1-4	Robertson	3195					6						1	2		3	10	5		9	4	7	8	11

68

1926/27

16th in Division Three (North)

#	Date	Opponent	Result	Scorers	Att	Ball S	Carlton J	Chester C	Chipperfield F	Clark JR	Dalkin AE	Dalkin JW	Elliott JW	Ferguson E	Grieve J	Hamilton G	Harris WJ	Johnson GA	Laverick W	Malloy W	Price J	Randall J	Ridley RH	Robinson C	Robson JW	Turnbull HW	Walls FB	Ward E	Watson WT
1	Aug 28	New Brighton	0-4		6146				6			7	1	2		3	4			9	5	10	8						11
2	Sep 4	WREXHAM	1-1	Malloy	1854				6			9	1	2		3	4			7	5	10	8						11
3	6	Walsall	0-0		5424				6			9	1	2		3	4		11	7	5	10	8						11
4	11	Wigan Borough	4-1	Harris 2, Watson, Johnson	2940			4	6			7	1	2		3	8	9			5	10							11
5	13	Nelson	0-4		5595				6			7	1	2		3	8	4			5	10			9				11
6	18	DONCASTER ROVERS	1-1	Harris	1672		4		6			7	1	2		3	8	9			5	10							11
7	25	Stoke City	0-7		8996				6			7	1	2		3	9	4			5	10	8						11
8	27	Chesterfield	1-4	Ward	4623				6			7	1	2		3	8	4			5	9						10	11
9	Oct 2	ROTHERHAM UNITED	4-4	Ward, Ferguson (p), JW Dalkin, Chipperfield	2022				6			7	1	2		3	4		11		5	9						8	10
10	9	Bradford Park Avenue	0-2		7080				6			7	1	2	5	3		9	11		4	8							10
11	16	ROCHDALE	2-2	Ferguson (p), Turnbull	2282				6			7	1	2	5	3	4					10				8			11
12	23	TRANMERE ROVERS	4-3	Johnson 2, Chipperfield, Robson	2025				6				1	2	5	3		8		7	4	10			9				11
13	30	ACCRINGTON STANLEY	2-1	Malloy, Robson	2048				6				1	2	5	3		8		7	4	10			9				11
14	Nov 6	Lincoln City	0-4		2733				6				1	2	5	3		8		7	4	10			9				11
15	13	HALIFAX TOWN	3-0	Price, Watson, Harris	1459			4	6					2		3	8	9		7	5	10	1						11
16	20	Barrow	2-2	Price, Chipperfield	3778			4	6					2		3	8	9		7	5	10	1						11
17	Dec 4	Hartlepools United	1-0	Harris	2062			4	6					2		3	8	9		7	5	10	1						11
18	18	Southport	1-4	Ferguson (p)	3418			4	6					2		3	8			7	5	10	1				9		11
19	25	Durham City	2-0	Malloy, Malloy	2496			4	6					2		3	8			7	5	10	1				9		11
20	27	Tranmere Rovers	1-2	Johnson	8322			4	6					2		3	8	9		7	5	10	1						11
21	Jan 1	DURHAM CITY	3-1	Malloy, Harris, Randall	3695			4	6					2		3	8	9		7		10	1	5					11
22	3	CHESTERFIELD	2-1	Grieve, Johnson	4635				6					2	5	3	8	9		7			1					4	11
23	15	NEW BRIGHTON	2-3	Johnson, Randall	3291				3					4	2		8	9		7	5	10	1					6	11
24	22	Wrexham	1-1	Harris	2874			4	6					2		3	8				5	10	1			7	9		11
25	29	WIGAN BOROUGH	1-1	Harris	2049			4						2		3	8	6			5	10	1			7	9		11
26	Feb 5	Doncaster Rovers	1-3	Harris	6336			4	6					2		3	8	10		7	5		1				9		11
27	12	STOKE CITY	0-2		6070				3					2		8		4		7	5	6	1	10	9				11
28	19	Rotherham United	0-5		3543				6					2		3	8	4		7	5	11	1				9		10
29	26	BRADFORD PARK AVE.	2-2	Harris 2	3499				6		4			2		3	8	10		7	5		1				9		11
30	Mar 5	Rochdale	0-5		2482				6		4			2		3	8	10		7	5		1				9		11
31	19	Accrington Stanley	0-3		3450	9			6	8	4			2		3				7	5	10	1						11
32	23	NELSON	1-1	Ball	1047	9			3	10	4			2				6		7	5	8	1						11
33	26	LINCOLN CITY	1-2	Watson	2623	9			6		4			2		3		10		7	5	8	1						11
34	Apr 2	Halifax Town	1-1	Ball	6253	9			6	10				2		3		4		7	5	8	1						11
35	4	WALSALL	0-2		630	9			6	10				2		3		4		7	5	8	1						11
36	9	BARROW	3-0	Ball 2, Watson	1678	9			6			7		2		3		4	11		5	8	1						10
37	11	STOCKPORT COUNTY	1-1	Watson	1521	9			6					2		3		4	11	7	5	8	1						10
38	16	Crewe Alexandra	1-2	Ball	4001	9			6		4			2		3			11	7	5	8	1						10
39	18	CREWE ALEXANDRA	4-1	Malloy, Ball 2, Chipperfield	1506	9	4		6					2		3			11	7	5	8	1						10
40	23	HARTLEPOOLS UNITED	1-0	Ball	1739	9			6		4			2		3			11	7	5	8	1						10
41	30	Stockport County	2-6	Laverick, Randall	5766	9			2	10	4					3		6	11	7	5	8	1						11
42	May 7	SOUTHPORT	4-1	Randall, Ball 2, Price	1544	9			6		4			2		3		10	11	7	5	8	1						11
				Apps		12	2	11	41	5	9	12	14	22	25	40	21	35	10	31	40	39	28	6	4	3	8	5	39
				Goals		10			4			1		3	1		11	6	1	6	3	4			2	1		2	5

F.A. Cup

#	Date	Opponent	Result	Scorers	Att	Ball S	Carlton J	Chester C	Chipperfield F	Clark JR	Dalkin AE	Dalkin JW	Elliott JW	Ferguson E	Grieve J	Hamilton G	Harris WJ	Johnson GA	Laverick W	Malloy W	Price J	Randall J	Ridley RH	Robinson C	Robson JW	Turnbull HW	Walls FB	Ward E	Watson WT
R1	Nov 27	Stockton	2-1	Watson, Randall	4500			4	6					2		3	8	9		7	5	10	1						11
R2	Dec 11	NELSON	2-1	Randall, Johnson	5265			4	6					2		3	8	9		7	5	10	1						11
R3	Jan 8	NOTTINGHAM FOREST	0-2		9242			4	6					2		3	8	9		7	5	10	1						11

1927/28

18th in Division Three (North)

#		Date	Opponent	Res	Scorers	Att	Ball S	Best E	Bradley W	Carlton J	Chipperfield F	Coombs JR	Ferguson E	Gaffney P	Graham E	Grieve J	Hamilton G	Hepple J	Hopper M	Johnson GA	Kirkup R	Laverick W	Moore D	Noble JF	Price J	Randall J	Richardson W	Ridley RH	Robinson C	Robinson GA	Robson JW	Turnbull HW	Watson WT
1	Aug	27	BRADFORD CITY	2-2	Randall, Ball	3841	9				6		2			4	3		7	8					5	10		1					11
2		29	CREWE ALEXANDRA	0-2		1825	9			4	6		2				3		7	8	1				5	10							11
3	Sep	3	New Brighton	0-6		5489	9			4	5		2				3		7	6	1					10						8	11
4		5	Halifax Town	1-6	Ball	4944	9			4			2	5			3			6	1					10			7			8	11
5		10	LINCOLN CITY	4-5	Ball,Watson,Johnson(p),Turnbull	3066	9	3	1	4	5						2		7	6						10						8	11
6		12	HALIFAX TOWN	3-3	Lees (og), Ball 2	1665	9	2	1	4	5						3		7	6						10						8	11
7		17	Hartlepools United	1-4	Ball	4294	9	2	1	4	5						3		7	6						10						8	11
8		24	ACCRINGTON STANLEY	1-1	Turnbull	2853	9	3	1	4	6								7	5						10					2	8	11
9	Oct	1	Wigan Borough	0-0		1696	9	3	1		8	6				5			7	4		11				10					2		
10		8	DONCASTER ROVERS	1-2	Johnson	2655	9	3	1		6					5			7	8		11			4	10					2		
11		15	Darlington	1-5	Ball	4902	9	3			6								7		4	11			5	8		1			2		10
12		22	Bradford Park Avenue	0-5		7315	8	3			6								7		4				5	11				2	9		10
13		29	CHESTERFIELD	0-0		2310	9	3			8	6							7		4				5	11		1			2		10
14	Nov	5	Wrexham	1-5	Randall	3531		3							9	6			7					8	5	11		1			2		10
15		12	TRANMERE ROVERS	3-0	Johnson, Randall, Graham	1785	9	3		4	6				8				7	5						11	2	1					10
16		19	Stockport County	0-3		6590		3		4	6				8				7	5						11	2	1		9			10
17	Dec	3	Nelson	5-1	Randall 2, Watson, Johnson 2	2936		3		4	6		2						7	9					5	11		1					10
18		10	BARROW	1-0	Randall	1680		3		4	6		2						7	9					5	11		1					10
19		17	Rotherham United	1-1	Johnson	4420		3		4	6		2						7	9					5	11		1					10
20		24	SOUTHPORT	1-3	Hopper	1703		3		4	6		2						7	9					5	11		1					10
21		31	Bradford City	0-5		5415				4	6		2		8		3			9					5	11		1	7				10
22	Jan	2	DURHAM CITY	2-2	Johnson 2	2099				4	6		2		8		3			9					5	11		1	7				10
23		7	NEW BRIGHTON	3-2	Graham, Johnson 2	1619				4	6		2		8		3			9						11		1	7				10
24		14	ROCHDALE	5-1	* see below	1223				4	6		2		8		3			9						11		1	7				10
25		21	Lincoln City	1-3	Watson	5768				4	6		2		8		3			9						11		1	7				10
26		28	HARTLEPOOLS UNITED	3-1	Robinson, Chipperfield, Randall	1407	8			4	6		2			5	3			9						11		1	7				10
27	Feb	4	Accrington Stanley	1-3	Johnson	2526	8			4	6		2			5	3			9						11		1	7				10
28		11	WIGAN BOROUGH	6-3	Ball 3, Johnson 3	1380	8	3		4	6		2			5				9						11		1	7				10
29		18	Doncaster Rovers	2-3	Ball, Robinson	6553				4	6		2			5	3			9						11		1	7				10
30		25	DARLINGTON	2-3	Ball 2	4232	9			4	6		2			5	3			8						11		1	7				10
31	Mar	3	BRADFORD PARK AVE.	0-3		4052	9			4	6		2				3			8					5	11		1	7				10
32		10	Chesterfield	0-3		2422		1		4	6		2		8	9	3								5	11			7				10
33		17	WREXHAM	2-1	Robinson, Chipperfield	1369	8	1		4	6		2				3			9					5	11			7				10
34		24	Tranmere Rovers	3-5	Watson, Randall 2	3749	8	1		4			2				3			10					5	11			7				6
35		31	STOCKPORT COUNTY	4-1	Watson 2, Randall, Johnson	2053	8	1		4	6				2		3			9					5	11			7				10
36	Apr	6	Crewe Alexandra	0-3		5874	8	1		4	6				2		3			9						11			7				10
37		7	Rochdale	2-2	Johnson, Robinson	3309	8	1		4	6				2		3			9						11			7				10
38		14	NELSON	5-1	Johnson 3, Randall, Robinson	1410	8	1		4	6		2				3			9						11			7				10
39		18	Durham City	0-0		931	8	1		4	6		2				3			9						11			7				10
40		21	Barrow	1-1	Graham	7273		1		4	6				8	2	3			9						11			7				10
41		28	ROTHERHAM UNITED	6-0	* see below	1464		1			6		2		8	4	3			9						11			7				10
42	May	5	Southport	3-3	Johnson, Johnson 2	1749		1			6		2		8	4	3			9						11			7				10
				Apps			27	17	17	20	38	18	26	1	14	16	27	2	19	37	5	3	3	1	28	42	2	22	23	7	2	6	39
				Goals			13				3				6					1	24					1	13			5			2	7

Two own goals

Scorers in game 24: Wood (og), Chipperfield, Johnson, Graham 2
Scorers in game 41: Graham, Johnson 2, Watson, Randall, Price

F.A. Cup

		Date	Opponent	Res	Scorers	Att	Ball S	Best E	Bradley W	Carlton J	Chipperfield F	Coombs JR	Ferguson E	Gaffney P	Graham E	Grieve J	Hamilton G	Hepple J	Hopper M	Johnson GA	Kirkup R	Laverick W	Moore D	Noble JF	Price J	Randall J	Richardson W	Ridley RH	Robinson C	Robinson GA	Robson JW	Turnbull HW	Watson WT
R1	Nov	26	Crewe Alexandra	2-2	Ball 2	4800	9	3		4	6				8				7	5						11	2	1					10
rep		30	CREWE ALEXANDRA	0-2		3000	9	3		4	6		2		8				7	5						11		1					10

1928/29

#	Date		Opponent	Score	Scorers	Att.	Alexander JW	Ball S	Bradley W	Carlton J	Charlton T	Chipperfield F	Clark H	Coombs JR	Dalkin AE	Dalkin JW	Grieve J	Harris WJ	Ions WT	Johnson GA	Latimer JG	Price J	Randall J	Richardson GE	Richardson W	Robson GA	Robson JW	Stephenson J	Stevens J	Taylor A	Thirlwell TW	Thompson G	Wilson T
1	Aug	25	Southport	1-2	Johnson	5151	7		1						6			8	10	9		5	11		2			3			4		
2		27	DARLINGTON	4-2	Randall 2, JW.Robson, Johnson	2540	7								6				10	9		5	11		2		8	3			4		
3	Sep	1	ROCHDALE	2-1	Johnson 2	3244	7		1						6				10	9		5	11		2		8	3			4		
4		8	New Brighton	2-3	Johnson 2	2821			1				7		6	8			10	9		5	11		2			3			4		
5		10	Stockport County	0-4		8908			1				7		6	8			10	9		5	11		2			3			4		
6		15	WREXHAM	2-2	Ions, Harris	2712			1			7			6		2	8	10	9		5	11					3			4		
7		19	Darlington	0-4		2861			1		6	7		8	4		2		10	9		5	11					3					
8		22	Chesterfield	1-4	Randall	4978			1		6	7		8	4		2		10	9		5	11					3					
9		29	BARROW	1-0	Johnson	2346			1		6	7			4		2		10	9		5	11				8	3					
10	Oct	6	Doncaster Rovers	1-2	JW.Robson	6783			1	8	6	7			4		2		10			5	11				9	3					
11		13	BRADFORD CITY	2-8	Randall, Carlton	2592	7		1	8	6				4		2		10	9		5	11					3					
12		20	Accrington Stanley	1-0	Johnson	3411	7		1		6				4			8	10	9		5		11	2			3					
13		27	HARTLEPOOLS UNITED	3-1	Johnson, E.Richardson 2	1419	7		1		4				6			8	10	9		5		11	2			3					
14	Nov	3	Carlisle United	1-5	Ions	6267	7		1		4				6			8	10	9		5		11	2			3					
15		10	ROTHERHAM UNITED	0-1		1626	7		1		4				6			8	10	9		5		11	2			3					
16		17	Wigan Borough	1-5	E.Richardson	4599	7		1	10	4				6					9		5		11	2		8	3					
17	Dec	1	Tranmere Rovers	2-3	Johnson, Stephenson (p)	4651	7		1	11	3				6				10	9		5					8	2					
18		8	Nelson	0-5		2915	7		1	11	3				6				10	9		5					8	2					4
19		15	Halifax Town	0-1		3422	7		1	8	3				6				10			5		11			9	2					4
20		22	LINCOLN CITY	1-1	JW.Robson	1129	7		1	11	3				6				10			5				8	9	2					4
21		25	SOUTH SHIELDS	1-3	JW.Robson	3245	7			11	3				6				10		1	5				8	9	2					4
22		26	South Shields	0-0		6328	7			11	3				6				10		1	5				8	9	2					4
23		29	SOUTHPORT	1-3	E.Richardson	1105	7				3				6				10		1	5		11			9	2					4
24	Jan	1	NELSON	3-2	JW.Robson 3	1344	7			6	3							8		9	1	5					10	2				
25		5	Rochdale	0-5		2464	7			10	3							8		9	1	5		11				2					6
26		12	CREWE ALEXANDRA	0-5		1166	7			4	3				6			8		9	1	5					10	2		11			
27		19	NEW BRIGHTON	1-1	Carlton	1344		8		10		6								9	1	5		11		2		3					4
28		26	Wrexham	0-4		3641		8		10		6								9	1	5		11		2		3					4
29	Feb	2	CHESTERFIELD	0-2		1039		8		10		6								9	1	5		11		2		3					4
30		9	Barrow	0-3		5628		8		11		6							10	9	1	5				2		3					4
31		16	DONCASTER ROVERS	4-7	Carlton 3, Johnson	729				10		6						8		9	1	5		11		2		3					4
32		23	Bradford City	0-2		16542	7			10		6						8		9	1	5		11		2		3					4
33	Mar	2	ACCRINGTON STANLEY	2-2	Carlton, E.Richardson	1124	7			10		6						8		9	1			11		2		3	5				4
34		9	Hartlepools United	3-1	Johnson 3	3398	7			10	3	6						8		9	1	5		11		2							4
35		16	CARLISLE UNITED	0-4		2219	7			10	3	6						8		9	1	5				2							4
36		23	Rotherham United	0-0		3078	7			10		6						8		9	1	5		11		2							4
37		30	WIGAN BOROUGH	1-1	Carlton	1226	7			10		6						8		9	1	5		11		2		3					4
38	Apr	1	Lincoln City	1-3	Harris	5068	7					6						8		9	1	5		11		2		3				10	4
39		6	Crewe Alexandra	0-7		2216	7	8		10		6								9	1	5		11		2		3					4
40		13	TRANMERE ROVERS	3-2	Alexander, Carlton, Johnson	725	7			10		6						8		9	1	5		11		2		3					4
41		20	STOCKPORT COUNTY	0-1		1399	7			10		6						8		9	1	5		11		2		3					4
42		27	HALIFAX TOWN	0-3		706	7			10		6						8		9	1	5		11		2		3					4
			Apps				29	5	19	27	17	24	2	8	26	14	6	19	21	32	22	41	11	23	10	14	15	42	2	1	6	1	22
			Goals				1			8								2	2	15			4	5				7	1				

Played in one game: JH Davison (game 8, at 8), AG Dixon (2, at 1), WR Elsdon (24, at 11)

F.A. Cup

R	Date		Opponent	Score		Att.	Alexander JW	Ball S	Bradley W	Carlton J	Charlton T	Chipperfield F	Clark H	Coombs JR	Dalkin AE	Dalkin JW	Grieve J	Harris WJ	Ions WT	Johnson GA	Latimer JG	Price J	Randall J	Richardson GE	Richardson W	Robson GA	Robson JW	Stephenson J	Stevens J	Taylor A	Thirlwell TW	Thompson G	Wilson T
R1	Nov	24	Wigan Borough	0-2		3956	7		1		4				6				10	9		5		11	2		8	3					

FOOTBALL LEAGUE DIVISION THREE (NORTH) 1921-22 TO 1928-29

1921-22

		home:					*away:*					*Tots:*		
	p	*w*	*d*	*l*	*f*	*a*	*w*	*d*	*l*	*f*	*a*	*f*	*a*	*pts*
1 Stockport County	38	13	5	1	36	10	11	3	5	24	11	60	21	56
2 Darlington	38	15	2	2	52	7	7	4	8	29	30	81	37	50
3 Grimsby Town	38	15	4	0	54	15	6	4	9	18	32	72	47	50
4 Hartlepools United	38	10	6	3	33	11	7	2	10	19	28	52	39	42
5 Accrington Stanley	38	15	1	3	50	15	4	2	13	23	42	73	57	41
6 Crewe Alexandra	38	13	1	5	39	21	5	4	10	21	35	60	56	41
7 Stalybridge Celtic	38	14	3	2	42	15	4	2	13	20	48	62	63	41
8 Walsall	38	15	2	2	52	17	3	1	15	14	48	66	65	39
9 Southport	38	11	6	2	39	12	3	4	12	16	32	55	44	38
10 ASHINGTON	38	13	2	4	42	22	4	2	13	17	44	59	66	38
11 Durham City	38	14	0	5	43	20	3	3	13	25	47	68	67	37
12 Wrexham	38	12	4	3	40	17	2	5	12	11	39	51	56	37
13 Chesterfield	38	12	2	5	33	15	4	1	14	15	52	48	67	35
14 Lincoln City	38	11	2	6	32	20	3	4	12	16	39	48	59	34
15 Barrow	38	11	2	6	29	18	3	3	13	13	36	42	54	33
16 Nelson	38	7	6	6	27	23	6	1	12	21	43	48	66	33
17 Wigan Borough	38	9	4	6	32	28	2	5	12	14	44	46	72	31
18 Tranmere Rovers	38	7	5	7	41	25	2	6	11	10	36	51	61	29
19 Halifax Town	38	9	4	6	37	28	1	5	13	19	48	56	76	29
20 Rochdale	38	9	2	8	34	24	2	2	15	18	53	52	77	26

1922-23

1 Nelson	38	15	2	2	37	10	9	1	9	24	31	61	41	51
2 Bradford Park Avenue	38	14	4	1	51	15	5	5	9	16	23	67	38	47
3 Walsall	38	13	4	2	32	14	6	4	9	19	30	51	44	46
4 Chesterfield	38	13	5	1	49	18	6	2	11	19	34	68	52	45
5 Wigan Borough	38	14	3	2	45	11	4	5	10	19	28	64	39	44
6 Crewe Alexandra	38	13	3	3	32	9	4	6	9	16	29	48	38	43
7 Halifax Town	38	11	4	4	29	14	6	3	10	24	32	53	46	41
8 Accrington Stanley	38	14	2	3	40	21	3	5	11	19	44	59	65	41
9 Darlington	38	13	3	3	43	14	2	7	10	16	32	59	46	40
10 Wrexham	38	13	5	1	29	12	1	5	13	9	36	38	48	38
11 Stalybridge Celtic	38	13	2	4	32	18	2	4	13	10	29	42	47	36
12 Rochdale	38	8	5	6	29	22	5	5	9	13	31	42	53	36
13 Lincoln City	38	9	7	3	21	11	4	3	12	18	44	39	55	36
14 Grimsby Town	38	10	3	6	35	18	4	2	13	20	34	55	52	33
15 Hartlepools United	38	10	6	3	34	14	0	6	13	14	40	48	54	32
16 Tranmere Rovers	38	11	4	4	41	21	1	4	14	8	38	49	59	32
17 Southport	38	11	3	5	21	12	1	4	14	11	34	32	46	31
18 Barrow	38	11	2	6	31	17	2	2	15	19	43	50	60	30
19 ASHINGTON	38	10	3	6	34	33	1	5	13	17	44	51	77	30
20 Durham City	38	7	9	3	31	19	2	1	16	12	40	43	59	28

1923-24

1 Wolverhampton Wan.	42	18	3	0	51	10	6	12	3	25	17	76	27	63
2 Rochdale	42	17	4	0	40	8	8	8	5	20	18	60	26	62
3 Chesterfield	42	16	4	1	54	15	6	6	9	16	24	70	39	54
4 Rotherham County	42	16	3	2	46	13	7	3	11	24	30	70	43	52
5 Bradford Park Avenue	42	17	3	1	50	12	4	7	10	19	31	69	43	52
6 Darlington	42	16	5	0	51	19	4	3	14	19	34	70	53	48
7 Southport	42	13	7	1	30	10	3	7	11	14	32	44	42	46
8 ASHINGTON	42	14	4	3	41	21	4	4	13	18	40	59	61	44
9 Doncaster Rovers	42	13	4	4	41	17	2	8	11	18	36	59	53	42
10 Wigan Borough	42	12	5	4	39	15	2	9	10	16	38	55	53	42
11 Grimsby Town	42	11	9	1	30	7	3	4	14	19	40	49	47	41
12 Tranmere Rovers	42	11	5	5	32	21	2	10	9	19	39	51	60	41
13 Accrington Stanley	42	12	5	4	35	21	4	3	14	13	40	48	61	40
14 Halifax Town	42	11	4	6	26	17	4	6	11	16	42	42	59	40
15 Durham City	42	12	5	4	40	23	3	4	14	19	37	59	60	39
16 Wrexham	42	8	11	2	24	12	2	7	12	13	32	37	44	38
17 Walsall	42	10	5	6	31	20	4	3	14	13	39	44	59	36
18 New Brighton	42	9	9	3	28	10	2	4	15	12	43	40	53	35
19 Lincoln City	42	8	8	5	29	22	2	4	15	19	37	48	59	32
20 Crewe Alexandra	42	6	7	8	20	24	1	6	14	12	34	32	58	27
21 Hartlepools United	42	5	7	9	22	24	2	4	15	11	46	33	70	25
22 Barrow	42	7	7	7	25	24	1	2	18	10	56	35	80	25

1924-25

1 Darlington	42	16	4	1	50	14	8	6	7	28	19	78	33	58
2 Nelson	42	18	2	1	58	14	5	5	11	21	36	79	50	53
3 New Brighton	42	17	3	1	56	16	6	4	11	19	34	75	50	53
4 Southport	42	17	2	2	41	7	5	5	11	18	30	59	37	51
5 Bradford Park Avenue	42	15	5	1	59	13	4	7	10	25	29	84	42	50
6 Rochdale	42	17	2	2	53	16	4	5	12	22	37	75	53	49
7 Chesterfield	42	14	3	4	42	15	3	8	10	18	29	60	44	45
8 Lincoln City	42	13	4	4	39	19	5	4	12	14	39	53	58	44
9 Halifax Town	42	11	5	5	36	22	5	6	10	20	30	56	52	43
10 ASHINGTON	42	13	4	4	41	24	3	6	12	27	52	68	76	42
11 Wigan Borough	42	10	7	4	39	16	5	4	12	23	49	62	65	41
12 Grimsby Town	42	10	6	5	38	21	5	3	13	22	39	60	60	39
13 Durham City	42	11	6	4	38	17	2	7	12	12	51	50	68	39
14 Barrow	42	14	4	3	39	22	2	3	16	12	52	51	74	39
15 Crewe Alexandra	42	11	7	3	35	24	2	6	13	18	54	53	78	39
16 Wrexham	42	11	5	5	37	21	4	3	14	16	40	53	61	38
17 Accrington Stanley	42	12	5	4	43	23	3	3	15	17	49	60	72	38
18 Doncaster Rovers	42	12	5	4	36	17	2	5	14	18	48	54	65	38
19 Walsall	42	10	6	5	27	16	3	5	13	17	37	44	53	37
20 Hartlepools United	42	9	8	4	28	21	3	3	15	17	42	45	63	35
21 Tranmere Rovers	42	11	3	7	40	29	3	1	17	19	49	59	78	32
22 Rotherham County	42	6	5	10	27	31	1	2	18	15	57	42	88	21

1925-26

		home:					*away:*					*Tots:*		
	p	*w*	*d*	*l*	*f*	*a*	*w*	*d*	*l*	*f*	*a*	*f*	*a*	*pts*
1 Grimsby Town	42	20	1	0	61	8	6	8	7	30	32	91	40	61
2 Bradford Park Avenue	42	18	2	1	65	10	8	6	7	36	33	101	43	60
3 Rochdale	42	16	1	4	55	25	11	4	6	49	33	104	58	59
4 Chesterfield	42	18	2	1	70	19	7	3	11	30	35	100	54	55
5 Halifax Town	42	12	5	4	34	19	5	6	10	19	31	53	50	45
6 Hartlepools United	42	15	5	1	59	23	3	3	15	23	50	82	73	44
7 Tranmere Rovers	42	15	2	4	45	27	4	4	13	28	56	73	83	44
8 Nelson	42	12	8	1	67	29	4	3	14	22	42	89	71	43
9 ASHINGTON	42	11	6	4	44	23	5	5	11	26	39	70	62	43
10 Doncaster Rovers	42	11	7	3	52	25	5	4	12	28	47	80	72	43
11 Crewe Alexandra	42	14	3	4	43	23	3	6	12	20	38	63	61	43
12 New Brighton	42	13	4	4	51	29	4	4	13	18	38	69	67	42
13 Durham City	42	14	5	2	45	19	4	1	16	18	51	63	70	42
14 Rotherham United	42	13	3	5	44	28	4	4	13	25	64	69	92	41
15 Lincoln City	42	14	2	5	42	28	3	3	15	24	54	66	82	39
16 Coventry City	42	13	6	2	47	19	3	0	18	26	63	73	82	38
17 Wigan Borough	42	12	5	4	53	22	1	6	14	15	52	68	74	37
18 Accrington Stanley	42	14	0	7	49	34	3	3	15	32	71	81	105	37
19 Wrexham	42	9	6	6	39	31	2	4	15	24	61	63	92	32
20 Southport	42	9	6	6	37	34	2	4	15	25	58	62	92	32
21 Walsall	42	9	4	8	40	34	1	2	18	18	73	58	107	26
22 Barrow	42	4	2	15	28	49	3	2	16	22	49	50	98	18

1926-27

1 Stoke City	42	17	3	1	57	11	10	6	5	35	29	92	40	63
2 Rochdale	42	18	2	1	72	22	8	4	9	33	43	105	65	58
3 Bradford Park Avenue	42	18	3	0	74	21	6	4	11	27	38	101	59	55
4 Halifax Town	42	13	6	2	46	23	8	5	8	24	30	70	53	53
5 Nelson	42	16	2	3	64	20	6	5	10	40	55	104	75	51
6 Stockport County	42	13	4	4	60	31	9	3	9	33	38	93	69	49
7 Chesterfield	42	15	4	2	65	24	6	1	14	27	44	92	68	47
8 Doncaster Rovers	42	13	4	4	58	27	5	7	9	23	38	81	65	47
9 Tranmere Rovers	42	13	5	3	54	22	6	3	12	31	45	85	67	46
10 New Brighton	42	14	2	5	49	21	4	8	9	30	46	79	67	46
11 Lincoln City	42	9	5	7	50	33	6	7	8	40	45	90	78	42
12 Southport	42	11	5	5	54	32	4	4	13	26	53	80	85	39
13 Wrexham	42	10	5	6	41	26	4	5	12	24	47	65	73	38
14 Walsall	42	10	4	7	35	22	4	6	11	33	59	68	81	38
15 Crewe Alexandra	42	11	5	5	46	28	3	4	14	25	53	71	81	37
16 ASHINGTON	42	9	8	4	42	30	3	4	14	18	60	60	90	36
17 Hartlepools United	42	11	4	6	43	26	3	2	16	23	55	66	81	34
18 Wigan Borough	42	10	6	5	44	28	1	4	16	22	55	66	83	32
19 Rotherham United	42	8	6	7	41	35	2	6	13	29	57	70	92	32
20 Durham City	42	9	4	8	35	35	3	2	16	23	70	58	105	30
21 Accrington Stanley	42	9	3	9	45	38	1	4	16	17	60	62	98	27
22 Barrow	42	5	6	10	22	40	2	2	17	12	77	34	117	22

1927-28

1 Bradford Park Avenue	42	18	2	1	68	22	9	7	5	33	23	101	45	63
2 Lincoln City	42	15	4	2	53	20	9	3	9	38	44	91	64	55
3 Stockport County	42	16	5	0	62	14	7	3	11	27	37	89	51	54
4 Doncaster Rovers	42	15	4	2	59	18	8	3	10	21	26	80	44	53
5 Tranmere Rovers	42	14	6	1	68	28	8	3	10	37	44	105	72	53
6 Bradford City	42	15	4	2	59	19	3	8	10	26	41	85	60	48
7 Darlington	42	15	1	5	63	28	6	4	11	26	46	89	74	47
8 Southport	42	15	2	4	55	24	5	3	13	24	46	79	70	45
9 Accrington Stanley	42	14	4	3	49	22	4	4	13	27	45	76	67	44
10 New Brighton	42	10	7	4	45	22	4	7	10	27	40	72	62	42
11 Wrexham	42	15	1	5	48	19	3	5	13	16	48	64	67	42
12 Halifax Town	42	11	7	3	47	24	2	8	11	26	47	73	71	41
13 Rochdale	42	13	4	4	45	24	4	3	14	29	53	74	77	41
14 Rotherham United	42	11	6	4	39	19	3	5	13	26	50	65	69	39
15 Hartlepools United	42	10	3	8	41	35	6	3	12	28	46	69	81	38
16 Chesterfield	42	10	4	7	46	29	3	6	12	25	49	71	78	36
17 Crewe Alexandra	42	10	6	5	51	28	2	4	15	26	58	77	86	34
18 ASHINGTON	42	10	5	6	54	36	1	6	14	23	67	77	103	33
19 Barrow	42	10	8	3	41	24	0	3	18	13	78	54	102	31
20 Wigan Borough	42	8	5	8	30	32	2	5	14	26	65	56	97	30
21 Durham City	42	10	5	6	37	30	1	2	18	16	70	53	100	29
22 Nelson	42	8	4	9	50	49	2	2	17	26	87	76	136	26

		home:						away:					Tots:		
		p	w	d	l	f	a	w	d	l	f	a	f	a	pts
1	Bradford City	42	17	2	2	82	18	10	7	4	46	25	128	43	63
2	Stockport County	42	19	2	0	77	23	9	4	8	34	35	111	58	62
3	Wrexham	42	17	2	2	59	25	4	8	9	32	44	91	69	52
4	Wigan Borough	42	16	4	1	55	16	5	5	11	27	33	82	49	51
5	Doncaster Rovers	42	14	3	4	39	20	6	7	8	37	46	76	66	50
6	Lincoln City	42	15	3	3	58	18	6	3	12	33	49	91	67	48
7	Tranmere Rovers	42	15	3	3	55	21	7	0	14	24	56	79	77	47
8	Carlisle United	42	15	3	3	61	27	4	5	12	25	50	86	77	46
9	Crewe Alexandra	42	11	6	4	47	23	7	2	12	33	45	80	68	44
10	South Shields	42	13	5	3	57	24	5	3	13	26	50	83	74	44
11	Chesterfield	42	13	2	6	46	28	5	3	13	25	49	71	77	41
12	Southport	42	13	5	3	52	27	3	3	15	23	58	75	85	40
13	Halifax Town	42	11	7	3	42	24	2	6	13	21	38	63	62	39
14	New Brighton	42	11	3	7	40	28	4	6	11	24	43	64	71	39
15	Nelson	42	14	1	6	48	28	3	4	14	29	62	77	90	39
16	Rotherham United	42	12	5	4	44	23	3	4	14	16	54	60	77	39
17	Rochdale	42	12	4	5	55	34	1	6	14	24	62	79	96	36
18	Accrington Stanley	42	11	5	5	42	22	2	3	16	26	60	68	82	34
19	Darlington	42	12	6	3	47	26	1	1	19	17	62	64	88	33
20	Barrow	42	7	6	8	42	37	3	2	16	22	56	64	93	28
21	Hartlepools United	42	9	4	8	35	38	1	2	18	24	74	59	112	26
22	ASHINGTON	42	6	5	10	31	52	2	2	17	14	63	45	115	23

OTHER NOTABLE LEAGUE SEASONS

Northern Alliance 1913-14

		p	w	d	l	f	a	pts
1	ASHINGTON	30	22	3	5	74	21	47
2	Birtley	30	18	9	3	58	21	45
3	Seaton Delaval	30	13	11	6	58	40	37
4	Newcastle East End	30	13	10	7	58	42	36
5	Spen Black & White	30	13	8	9	61	40	34
6	Annfield Plain	30	13	6	11	66	53	32
7	Bedlington	30	10	11	9	40	35	31
8	Hexham Athletic	30	13	5	12	43	46	31
9	Newburn	30	9	11	10	47	49	29
10	Scotswood	30	11	7	12	53	61	29
11	Benwell Adelaide	30	9	9	12	41	48	27
12	Mickley	30	9	9	12	33	37	27
13	New Hartley	30	10	6	14	35	60	26
14	Wellington Athletic	30	7	8	15	43	76	22
15	Choppington	30	8	3	19	46	67	19
16	Parkside	30	2	3	25	21	80	7

Northern Premier League 1968-69

1	Macclesfield Town	38	27	6	5	82	38	60
2	Wigan Athletic	38	18	12	8	59	41	48
3	Morecambe	38	16	14	8	64	37	46
4	Gainsborough Trinity	38	19	8	11	64	43	46
5	South Shields	38	19	8	11	78	56	46
6	Bangor City	38	18	9	11	102	64	45
7	Hyde United	38	16	10	12	71	65	42
8	Goole Town	38	15	10	13	80	78	40
9	Altrincham	38	14	10	14	69	52	38
10	Fleetwood	38	16	6	16	58	58	38
11	Gateshead	38	14	9	15	42	48	37
12	South Liverpool	38	12	13	13	56	66	37
13	Northwich Victoria	38	16	5	17	59	82	37
14	Boston United	38	14	8	16	59	65	36
15	Runcorn	38	12	11	15	59	63	35
16	Netherfield	38	12	4	22	51	69	28
17	Scarborough	38	9	10	19	49	68	28
18	ASHINGTON	38	10	8	20	48	74	28
19	Chorley	38	8	9	21	46	75	25
20	Worksop Town	38	6	8	24	34	88	20

The Northern Premier League is the highest level at which Ashington have played since 1929. Five of these clubs went on to play in the Football League and one reached the Premiership

Northern League Division Two 2000-01

		p	w	d	l	f	a	pts
1	ASHINGTON	36	25	5	6	100	41	80
2	Washington IH	36	23	10	3	83	35	79
3	Thornaby	36	23	7	6	85	50	76
4	Horden CW	36	20	7	9	53	35	67
5	Esh Winning	36	19	7	10	79	44	64
6	Northallerton Town	36	16	12	8	78	48	60
7	Penrith	36	14	12	10	60	52	54
8	Norton	36	16	9	11	51	51	57
9	Willington	36	12	12	12	52	46	48
10	Kennek Ryhope CA	36	12	10	14	46	53	46
11	South Shields	36	12	9	15	71	81	45
12	Prudhoe Town	36	13	5	18	69	66	44
13	Shildon	36	12	8	16	42	58	44
14	Alnwick Town	36	9	12	15	53	61	39
15	Evenwood Town	36	10	5	21	50	97	35
16	Shotton Comrades	36	8	10	18	49	85	34
17	Murton	36	9	8	19	53	76	35
18	Whickham	36	6	11	19	43	68	29
19	Eppleton CW	36	1	5	30	29	99	8

Northern League Division Two 2003-04

1	ASHINGTON	38	27	7	4	91	28	88
2	Newc. Benfield Saints	38	26	7	5	106	42	85
3	Consett	38	25	8	5	84	35	83
4	Newc. Blue Star	38	24	6	8	87	53	75 (-3)
5	Washington Nissan	38	21	6	11	81	47	69
6	Prudhoe Town	38	18	4	16	73	70	58
7	Northallerton Town	38	15	12	11	73	57	57
8	Hebburn Town	38	16	6	16	64	58	54
9	Kennek Ryhope CA	38	15	8	15	65	55	53
10	Whickham	38	14	10	14	66	57	52
11	Alnwick Town	38	15	6	17	50	59	51
12	South Shields	38	14	8	16	61	68	50
13	Seaham Red Star	38	11	10	17	73	78	43
14	Evenwood Town	38	13	4	21	43	58	43
15	Murton	38	11	9	18	58	68	42
16	Crook Town	38	11	8	19	61	79	41
17	Willington	38	11	5	22	50	104	38
18	Norton & Stockton Ancs	38	10	5	23	49	89	35
19	Easington Colliery	38	8	3	27	41	119	27
20	Shotton Comrades	38	6	6	26	47	99	24

ASHINGTON IN THE FA CUP

The year is the final year of the season; i.e. 1920 is season 1919-20

1889	Q1	Ashington	0	Elswick Rangers	4	1924	Q4	Ashington	2	Bishop Auckland	1
							Q5	Ashington	2	Carlisle United	0
1891	Q2	Shankhouse	2	Ashington	0		Q6	Ashington	2	Hartlepools United	1
							R1	Ashington	1	Aston Villa	5
1892	Q1	Gateshead NER	7	Ashington	2						
						1925	Q4	Hartlepools United	0	Ashington	0
1893	Q1	Tow Law	3	Ashington	3 d		Q4 r	Ashington	2	Hartlepools United	0 D
1900	PR	Ashington	0	St Peter's Albion	1	1926	R1	Durham City	4	Ashington	1
1904	Q1	Morpeth Harriers	1	Ashington	1	1927	R1	Stockton	1	Ashington	2
	Q1 r	Ashington	1	Morpeth Harriers	2		R2	Ashington	2	Nelson	1
							R3	Ashington	0	Nottingham Forest	2
1905	Q1	Ashington	1	Shankhouse	3						
						1928	R1	Crewe Alexandra	2	Ashington	2
1907	PR	Ashington	3	Gateshead Town	0		R1 r	Ashington	0	Crewe Alexandra	2
	Q1	Ashington	2	North Shields Ath.	2						
	Q1 r	North Shields Ath.	2	Ashington	1	1929	R1	Wigan Borough	2	Ashington	0
1908	PR	Hebburn Argyle	3	Ashington	1	1930	Q4	Ashington	4	Stockton	0
							R1	Rotherham United	3	Ashington	0
1909	PR	North Shields Ath.	4	Ashington	0						
						1931	PR	Walker Celtic	3	Ashington	0
1910	PR	Walker Parish Church	2	Ashington	2						
	PR r	Ashington	3	Walker Parish Church	1	1932	PR	North Shields	2	Ashington	1
	Q1	North Shields Ath.	4	Ashington	5						
	Q2	Bedlington United	3	Ashington	0	1933	PR	Wallsend	2	Ashington	0
1911	PR	Mickley	0	Ashington	2	1934	EP	West Wylam CW	1	Ashington	1
	Q1	Blaydon United	0	Ashington	4		EP r	Ashington	8	West Wylam CW	2
	Q2	Newburn	3	Ashington	1		PR	Ashington	2	Birtley	0
							Q1	Rosehill	1	Ashington	1
1912	PR	Ashington	5	Mickley	2		Q1 r	Ashington	3	Rosehill	1
	Q1	Jarrow Croft	0	Ashington	0		Q2	Ashington	0	Blyth Spartans	0
	Q1 r	Ashington	0	Jarrow Croft	3		Q2 r	Blyth Spartans	1	Ashington	1
							Q2 r2	Blyth Spartans	2	Ashington	1
1913	EP	Ashington	5	Birtley	2						
	PR	Blyth Spartans	3	Ashington	0	1935	PR	Ashington	2	Dipton United	2
							PR r	Dipton United	2	Ashington	1
1914	EP	Mickley	0	Ashington	2						
	PR	Willington Athletic	1	Ashington	3	1936	EP	Ashington	5	Newburn	3
	Q1	Ashington	1	Blyth Spartans	1		PR	Ashington	0	Walker Celtic	2
	Q1 r	Blyth Spartans	1	Ashington	2						
	Q2	Ashington	4	Newcastle City	3	1937	EP	Ashington	3	Usworth Colliery	0
	Q3	Jarrow	0	Ashington	0		PR	Ashington	7	Crawcrook Albion	1
	Q3 r	Ashington	2	Jarrow	0		Q1	Ashington	2	Jarrow	0
	Q4	Ashington	1	Willington	1		Q2	Ashington	1	Birtley	2
	Q4 r	Willington	4	Ashington	0						
						1938	PR	Ashington	4	Newburn	1
1915	PR	Spen Black & White	1	Ashington	0		Q1	Ashington	0	Annfield Plain	1
1920	PR	Ashington	1	Close Works	0	1939	EP	Crookhall CW	2	Ashington	1
	Q1	Ashington	4	Pandon Temperance	0						
	Q2	Ashington	0	Blyth Spartans	3	1940	EP	Ashington	2	Whitley & Monkseaton	1
1921	PR	Ashington	1	Close Works	0	1946	Q1	Annfield Plain	1	Ashington	2
	Q1	Ashington	2	Spen Black & White	0		Q2	Ashington	1	Consett	1
	Q2	Ashington	0	Wallsend	1		Q2 r	Consett	3	Ashington	0
1922	Q4	Close Works	0	Ashington	6						
	Q5	Ashington	2	Leadgate Park	1						
	Q6	Ashington	1	Stalybridge Celtic	0						
	R1	Millwall	4	Ashington	2						
1923	Q5	Blyth Spartans	2	Ashington	1						

Year	Round					
1947	Q1	Murton CW	1	Ashington	3	
	Q2	Newburn	3	Ashington	3	
	Q2 r	Ashington	6	Newburn	1	
	Q3	Ashington	7	Crook CW	1	
	Q4	North Shields	1	Ashington	1	
	Q4 r	Ashington	1	North Shields	1	x
	Q4 r2	North Shields	3	Ashington	1	
1948	Q1	Ashington	4	West Stanley	3	
	Q2	South Shields	3	Ashington	1	
1949	PR	Ashington	1	West Stanley	0	
	Q1	Blyth Spartans	2	Ashington	1	
1950	EP	Ashington	5	Wardley Welfare	2	
	PR	Alnwick Town	2	Ashington	4	
	Q1	Ashington	2	Heaton Stannington	3	
1951	PR	Ashington	3	Annfield Plain	1	
	Q1	Ashington	2	West Stanley	1	
	Q2	Ashington	0	Hexham Hearts	0	
	Q2 r	Hexham Hearts	2	Ashington	6	
	Q3	Ashington	3	Cramlington Welfare	1	
	Q4	Ashington	2	Farsley Celtic	1	
	R1	Halifax Town	2	Ashington	3	
	R2	Ashington	1	Rochdale	2	
1952	Q4	Ashington	0	Blyth Spartans	2	
1953	Q1	Amble	0	Ashington	4	
	Q2	Hexham Hearts	3	Ashington	5	
	Q3	Newburn	1	Ashington	4	
	Q4	Ashington	4	Billingham Synthonia	0	
	R1	Tranmere Rovers	8	Ashington	1	
1954	Q1	Ashington	1	West Sleekburn Welfare	2	
1955	PR	Newburn	1	Ashington	6	
	Q1	Ashington	6	Heaton Stannington	1	
	Q2	Ashington	2	North Shields	0	
	Q3	Ashington	2	West Sleekburn Welfare	1	
	Q4	Ashington	2	Scarborough	3	
1956	Q1	Ashington	7	Gosforth & Coxlodge	0	
	Q2	North Shields	3	Ashington	1	
1957	Q1	Whitley Bay	1	Ashington	3	
	Q2	North Shields	1	Ashington	0	
1958	Q2	North Shields	0	Ashington	0	
	Q2 r	Ashington	3	North Shields	1	
	Q3	Horden CW	3	Ashington	1	
1959	Q2	Consett	3	Ashington	2	
1960	Q1	Scarborough	2	Ashington	2	
	Q1 r	Ashington	0	Scarborough	0	
	Q1 r2	Scarborough	1	Ashington	0	N
1961	Q1	Ashington	2	Newburn	1	
	Q2	Ashington	6	Silksworth CW	1	
	Q3	Ferryhill Athletic	2	Ashington	1	
1962	PR	Ashington	3	Spennymoor United	2	
	Q1	Ashington	4	Silksworth CW	1	
	Q2	Stanley United	1	Ashington	4	
	Q3	Ashington	2	Bedlington Mechanics	2	
	Q3 r	Bedlington Mechanics	1	Ashington	4	
	Q4	Scarborough	2	Ashington	2	
	Q4 r	Ashington	2	Scarborough	0	
	R1	Chester	4	Ashington	1	
1963	Q1	Ashington	4	Willington	3	
	Q2	Stockton	wo	Ashington	scr	
1964	Q1	Ashington	1	Billingham Synthonia	1	
	Q1 r	Billingham Synthonia	0	Ashington	2	
	Q2	Stanley United	3	Ashington	0	
1965	Q2	Ashington	0	Tow Law Town	0	
	Q2 r	Tow Law Town	0	Ashington	0	
	Q2 r2	Ashington	1	Tow Law Town	2	
1966	Q1	Ashington	3	West Auckland Town	1	
	Q2	Stockton	3	Ashington	1	
1967	Q1	Ashington	2	North Shields	2	
	Q1 r	North Shields	2	Ashington	4	
	Q2	Horden CW	2	Ashington	1	
1968	Q1	Ashington	3	Horden CW	2	
	Q2	West Auckland Town	0	Ashington	1	
	Q3	Tow Law Town	3	Ashington	2	
1969	Q1	Billingham Synthonia	2	Ashington	0	
1970	Q1	Ryhope CW	0	Ashington	1	
	Q2	Bishop Auckland	3	Ashington	0	
1973	Q1	Crook Town	2	Ashington	0	
1974	Q1	Billingham Synthonia	1	Ashington	4	
	Q2	Ashington	2	Murton CW	1	
	Q3	Horden CW	1	Ashington	1	
	Q3 r	Ashington	2	Horden CW	1	
	Q4	Willington	1	Ashington	0	
1975	Q1	Ashington	2	Horden CW	1	
	Q2	Tow Law Town	0	Ashington	4	
	Q3	Ashington	2	Willington	2	
	Q3 r	Willington	1	Ashington	5	
	Q4	Ashington	1	Gateshead United	3	
1976	Q1	Ashington	0	Netherfield (Kendal)	2	
1979	Q1	Ashington	0	Bishop Auckland	1	
1980	Q1	Boldon CA	0	Ashington	1	
	Q2	Crook Town	2	Ashington	3	
	Q3	North Shields	2	Ashington	1	
1981	Q1	Ashington	0	Bishop Auckland	3	
1982	Q1	Ashington	4	Crook Town	2	
	Q2	Lancaster City	1	Ashington	3	
	Q3	Horden CW	0	Ashington	0	
	Q3 r	Ashington	1	Horden CW	3	e
1983	PR	Ashington	2	Chester-le-Street T	2	
	PR r	Chester-le-Street T	2	Ashington	1	

Year	Round	Home		Away	
1984	PR	Durham City	3	Ashington	1
1985	Q1	Ashington	3	Whitley Bay	1
	Q2	Ashington	0	Bishop Auckland	5
1986	PR	Ashington	0	Durham City	2
1987	PR	Ashington	3	Seaham Red Star	2
	Q1	Ashington	2	Bridlington Town	4
1988	PR	Ashington	3	Guiseley	1
	Q1	Ryhope CA	1	Ashington	1
	Q1 r	Ashington	1	Ryhope CA	2
1989	PR	Ashington	2	Rossendale United	4
1990	PR	Harworth Coll. Inst.	0	Ashington	3
	Q1	Ashington	0	Alnwick Town	5
1991	PR	Ashington	1	Prudhoe East End	4
1992	PR	Ashington	3	Crook Town	1
	Q1	Ashington	0	Consett	4
1997	PR	Ashington	4	Ashfield United	5
1998	Q1	Ashington	0	Farsley Celtic	2
1999	PR	Ashington	2	Horden CW	1 e
	Q1	Ashington	0	Louth United	2
2000	PR	Marske United	1	Ashington	1
	PR r	Ashington	1	Marske United	2
2001	PR	Whitley Bay	2	Ashington	1
2002	PR	Warrington Town	0	Ashington	0
	PR r	Ashington	3	Warrington Town	0
	Q1	Ramsbottom United	6	Ashington	1
2003	PR	Ashington	7	Colne	0
	Q1	Spennymoor United	1	Ashington	1
	Q1 r	Ashington	1	Spennymoor United	2
2004	PR	Maine Road	2	Ashington	4
	Q1	Ashington	3	Ramsbottom United	1
	Q2	Maltby Main	2	Ashington	3
	Q3	Ashington	1	Grantham Town	3
2005	PR	North Shields	0	Ashington	1
	Q1	West Auckland Town	0	Ashington	2
	Q2	Ashington	1	Droylsden	3
2006	EP	Esh Winning	4	Ashington	4
	EP r	Ashington	1	Esh Winning	0
	PR	Pickering Town	2	Ashington	2
	PR r	Ashington	1	Pickering Town	2
2007	EP	Ashington	0	Thornaby	0
	EP r	Thornaby	3	Ashington	2
2008	EP	Thackley	0	Ashington	1
	PR	Ashington	1	Newcastle Blue Star	3
2009	EP	Ashington	1	Thackley	0
	PR	Ashington	2	Ossett Albion	1
	Q1	Ashington	0	Durham City	6
2010	EP	Spennymoor Town	5	Ashington	1
2011	EP	Ashington	4	Billingham Town	1
	PR	Wakefield	2	Ashington	3
	Q1	Ashington	3	Northallerton T	1
	Q2	Ashington	1	Thackley	0
	Q3	Ashington	1	Droylsden	4

FA AMATEUR CUP

Year	Round	Home		Away	
1894	Q2	Kendal	2	Ashington	4
	Q3	Willington Athletic	4	Ashington	0
1970	PR	Ashington	5	Winlaton Mill Athletic	2
	Q1	Billingham Synthonia	3	Ashington	1
1971	PR	Ashington	0	Consett	1
1972	Q1	Ashington	0	Consett	1
1973	Q1	Ashington	5	Annan Athletic	2
	Q2	Ashington	1	Stanley United	0
	Q3	Ashington	4	Consett	1
	Q4	North Ferriby United	2	Ashington	2
	Q4 r	Ashington	1	North Ferriby United	0
	R1	Ashington	0	Alvechurch	1
1974	PR	Ashington	2	Wingate (Durham)	1
	Q1	Ashington	5	Wallsend	2
	Q2	Durham City	0	Ashington	1
	Q3	Consett	0	Ashington	1
	Q4	Ashington	2	Whitley Bay	0
	R1	Marine	1	Ashington	2
	R2	Slough Town	1	Ashington	1
	R2 r	Ashington	1	Slough Town	0
	R3	Ashington	1	North Shields	1
	R3 r	North Shields	0	Ashington	2
	R4	Ashington	2	Woking	0
	SF	Bishops Stortford	0	Ashington	0 N
	SF r	Bishops Stortford	3	Ashington	0 N

FA TROPHY

Year	Round	Home		Away	
1975	Q3	Ashington	0	Blyth Spartans	1
1976	Q3	Ashington	3	North Shields	2
1976	R1	Ashington	2	Goole Town	2
1976	R1 r	Goole Town	3	Ashington	1
1979	Q2	Horwich RMI	3	Ashington	0
1980	Q3	Whitby Town	1	Ashington	3
1980	R1	Crook Town	2	Ashington	3
1980	R2	Ashington	0	Woking	2
1981	R1	Nuneaton Borough	1	Ashington	2
1981	R2	Dartford	1	Ashington	0
1982	R1	Ashington	1	Blyth Spartans	2
1983	R1	Ashington	1	Burscough	0
1983	R2	Ashington	1	Barrow	1
1983	R2 r	Barrow	1	Ashington	0
1984	Q3	Spennymoor United	2	Ashington	1
1985	Q1	Whitley Bay	3	Ashington	0

FA VASE

1986	PR	Ashington	2 West Allotment Celtic	3		
1987	PR	Ashington	2 Evenwood Town	1		
	R1	Annfield Plain	2 Ashington	3		
	R2	Ashington	1 Garforth Town	5		
1988	PR	Ashington	2 Norton & Stockton Anc.	1		
	R1	Murton	1 Ashington	2		
	R2	Thackley	6 Ashington	0		
1989	PR	Clitheroe	3 Ashington	2		
1990	PR	Peterlee Newtown	3 Ashington	2		
1991	PR	Ashington	3 Cleator Moor Celtic	1		
	R1	Ashington	1 Hebburn	0 v		
	R1 r	Ashington	3 Hebburn	0		
	R2	Langley Park	0 Ashington	1		
	R3	Cammell Laird	1 Ashington	1		
	R3 r	Ashington	0 Cammell Laird	3		
1992	PR	Ashington	1 Penrith	2		
1996	Q2	Ashington	3 Darl'n Cleveland Social	0		
	R1	Ashington	0 North Ferriby United	3		
1997	Q1	Ashington	2 Tadcaster Albion	3 e		
1998	Q2	Harrogate Railway A.	0 Ashington	5		
	R1	Poulton Victoria	4 Ashington	2		
1999	Q2	South Shields	1 Ashington	0		
2000	Q2	Glasshoughton Welf.	2 Ashington	1		
2001	Q2	Ashington	1 Billingham Town	3		
2002	Q1	West Auckland Town	5 Ashington	2		
2003	Q2	Alnwick Town	0 Ashington	7		
	R1	Horden CW	1 Ashington	0 e		
2004	Q1	Evenwood Town	2 Ashington	4 N		
	Q2	Atherton LR	0 Ashington	1		
	R1	Hall Road Rangers	2 Ashington	1		
2005	Q2	Shildon	3 Ashington	2 e		
2006	Q2	South Shields	1 Ashington	3		
	R1	Ashington	3 Thornaby	3 e		
	R1 r	Thornaby	4 Ashington	3		
2007	Q2	Northallerton Town	0 Ashington	1		
	R1	Ashington	1 Durham City	3		
2008	Q1	Crook Town	2 Ashington	1 e		
2009	Q2	Ashington	2 North Shields	0		
	R1	Ashington	3 Leeds Carnegie	1		
	R2	Winterton Rangers	3 Ashington	1 e		
2010	Q2	Ashington	0 Armthorpe Welfare	1		

2011	Q1	Ashington	4 Whickham	0
	Q2	Morpeth Town	0 Ashington	5
	R1	Billingham Town	3 Ashington	4
	R2	New Mills AFC	2 Ashington	4
	R3	Dunkirk	1 Ashington	2
	R4	Long Buckby	3 Ashington	2

ABOUT THE AUTHOR

Garth Dykes was born at Mellor, near Blackburn, and was educated at Chadderton Grammar School. Qualifications in cotton spinning followed, and a career in yarn sales commenced in 1957. A career move took Garth to Leicestershire in 1961 and he retired in 1992 at the age of 58. A member of the Football Writers' Association, Garth attended his first match at Boundary Park, Oldham, in season 1945-46, and his lifelong love of football has seen his involvement in fifteen books to date.

BY THE SAME AUTHOR

Oldham Athletic-A Complete Record, 1899-1988 (Breedon Books)

Exeter City-A Complete Record, 1904-1990, with Alex Wilson and Maurice Golesworthy (Breedon Books 1990)

New Brighton-A Complete Record of the Rakers in the Football League, (Breedon Books 1990)

Accrington Stanley-A Complete Record, 1894-1962, with Mike Jackman (Breedon Books 1991)

The United Alphabet-A Complete Who's Who of Manchester United F.C. (ACL and Polar Publishing (UK) Ltd. 1994)

All The Lads-A Complete Who's Who of Sunderland A.F.C., with Doug Lamming (Polar Publishing 1999)

Latics Lads-The Official Who's Who of Oldham Athletic A.F.C. 1907-2002 (Yore Publications 2002)

Meadow Lane Men-The Complete Who's Who of Notts County F.C., 1888-2005 (Yore Publications 2005)

The Legends of Oldham Athletic (Breedon Books 2006)

The Who's Who of Oldham Athletic (Breedon Books 2008)

The Who's Who of Barrow A.F.C.-Barrow's Football League Players 1921-1972 (Soccerdata 2009)

Nelson F.C. in the Football League. A Complete Record and Who's Who 1921-31 (Soccerdata 2009)

Durham City in the Football League. A Complete Record and Who's Who 1921-28 (Soccerdata 2010)

A Spinner's Yarn. High Crompton St Mary's C.C. The Official History 1904-2010, with Allan Cadman (Soccerdata 2010)

Also in this complete record series by Garth Dykes, Nelson FC and Durham City FC. Each book is priced at £10 plus £1.50 postage, and can be obtained from the publisher Tony Brown